The Minarets of Cairo

"The city of Cairo
stretched out in its
maiden glory
among orchards and palms,
while the four hundred voices
from the minarets
called the believers to prayer,
and rose like incense
to the Lord of all."

Arabian Nights, "Tales of the two lives
of Sultan Muhammad"

Doris Behrens-Abouseif

The Minarets of Cairo

*Photographs
By Muhammad Yusuf*

The American University in Cairo Press

Funded by the Aga Khan Program for Islamic Architecture at Harvard University and the Massachussetts Institute of Technology.

Dar el Kutub No. 3815/84
ISBN 977 424 035 9

Printed in Egypt at the Printshop of the American University in Cairo Press

Contents

Acknowledgments

I would like to thank the director of the Registration Office for Islamic and Coptic Antiquities for providing most of the plans of the minarets included in this book. My thanks also go to the Minister of Waqf and the Director of the National Archives (Dar al-Watha'iq al-Qawmiyya) for permission to study waqf documents of the Mamluk and Ottoman periods. I also thank the Curator of the Creswell Library at the American University in Cairo for having allowed me to use albums of K.A.C. Creswell's photographs.

Mr Mukhtar Saleh earns my gratitude for advice in matters of technical architectural interest; and Mr Husam al-Din Ismail and Mr Rifaat Musa for their assistance in the difficult task of reading inscriptions on minarets.

To Dr. John Rodenbeck I am grateful for helping me with the challenging task of writing in English.

I am very grateful to the Aga Khan Program for Islamic Architecture at Harvard University and the Massachussetts Institute of Technology for sponsoring both the research and the publication of this book.

And in appreciation for her generous help and advice I dedicate this work to Ms Layla Ali Ibrahim.

Preface

An important number of historic monuments have disappeared in modern Cairo, particularly in the last decades of the city's explosive expansion. Today, most of the monuments of the old city are disappearing, if not physically, then visually behind the concrete masses of highrise buildings that have altered the proportions of Cairo's traditional skyline. Most of the photographs of this book were taken during the year 1982. It was not an easy task for M. Muhammad Yusuf, chief photographer at the newspaper al-Ahram, because so many minarets are squeezed between modern buildings; and yet, today—1984—the same task would be even more difficult. It was urgent to make a survey of the historic minarets of Cairo, before it became too late. In fact, during my work on this survey one of the Mamluk minarets—that of Amir Husayn—was on the verge of collapsing, and the Department of Antiquities had shored it up with scaffolds before we had time to make a photograph of it; I had to use an old photograph instead.

The aim of this book is to present a survey of the minarets of Cairo in their number and variety before more of them are lost. I have tried to give as much information as possible concerning the function and meaning of the minaret in the urban context of the medieval capital. It is not within the scope of this work to deal with all the architectural and archeological problems of each single minaret, nor to include a study of their decoration. It was, however, necessary to present their Koranic inscriptions, never published before as a whole, while they are still legible and before pollution and decay increase the damage to the old stones.

7

Background to the Survey

Since the beginning of its history, architecture has been the greatest expression of Egyptian civilization. Two Egyptian architectural achievements were honored by the Greeks among their seven world wonders—the Pyramids of Giza and the Pharos of Alexandria.

Cairene architecture reflects the tastes of a cosmopolitan society. During the centuries after the establishment of an Islamic Egypt, numbers of races and peoples settled within the small area between Fustat and al-Qahira; and to the native Copts came Arabs, Berbers, Sudanese, Ethiopians, Turks, Circassians, Kurds, Mongols, Albanians, Greeks and Slavs, adding and mixing traditions and tastes within the same Islamic frame. Located between Eastern and Western Islam, between Asia and Europe, medieval Egypt lived and prospered on transit trade, which meanwhile brought other international influence. Politics also played a role. As long as Damascus, Baghdad and Samarra ruled the Islamic empire, their fashions ruled in Egypt as elsewhere in the empire. Thus the mosque of Fustat was decorated with mosaics and had four minarets like the Great Mosque at Damascus, while the mosque of Ibn Tulun shows what the mosque of Samarra may have looked like.

With the foundation of al-Qahira as capital and residence of the Fatimid Caliphs, a royal style was again created in Egypt, a style that drew upon both local and foreign traditions and flourished until the end of the Mamluk rule. Ambitious sultans and amirs throughout the centuries crowded the capital and its suburbs with pious and religious edifices. No matter what their real motives were—and benevolence and piety were frequently less important than glory or material gain—the heritage is a great one, as can still be seen despite neglect and decay.

If the dome and the minaret are the most immediate and characteristic features of Islamic architecture, carved stone domes and three-storied minarets are the landmarks of Cairo. Rectangular, circular, octagonal, hexagonal, facetted, spiral or tapering, Cairene minarets display all the shapes a tower can possibly have. From Ibn Tulun to al-Hakim, from Qalawun to Qaytbay, their forms have constantly evolved, sometimes regularly and sometimes—with the appearance of "disturbing elements" or even of archaisms—unexpectedly.

Major buildings have disappeared and a study of this evolution can therefore never be quite true or complete, particularly when one is dealing with exceptions. One can say, however, that the principle that ruled medieval Islamic architecture, and ruled probably more in Cairo than in most other Islamic capitals, was variation. Variation in Cairo was dictated primarily by the heavy concentration of buildings within the same area, which made the achievement of distinction both difficult and highly desirable. This urban density is what made the distinctive treatment of external architectural features so important.

The minaret

The most prominent external feature of a religious building in Cairo is the minaret. Unlike the dome, it is linked to a function without which the mosque could not properly fulfill its purpose as a place of prayer. Functionally, the minaret is an elevated structure intended for the use of the *mu'adhdhin* as he summons people to fulfill this duty. Even in the days of the Prophet it was necessary for Bilal, the first *mu'adhdhin* of Islam, to climb to a high place to be heard, using an elevated structure for the call to prayer. This structure—said to be movable and traditionally described as circular—was the forerunner of the minaret and had its parallel in the pulpit used by the Prophet and his successors to be heard by the crowds gathered for the Friday sermon. It is the purpose of the *adhan* (prayer call), and the range of the human voice, that in theory dictate the maximum and minimum height of a minaret, since sufficient height is necessary, while too much height would allow the call to dissipate before reaching its audience.

A scholar of the French Expedition in Egypt described the minaret as the bell-tower of the Muslims, "*le clocher des Mohametans*". This definition is not inapt. By announcing prayer time, the *mu'adhdhin* on the minaret also announces the time of day. Even today in areas where not everyone possesses a watch, it is the *adhan* that indicates the hour, and people make their appointments "after the 'isha" or "before the *zuhr*". Thus, while indicating the prayer time for those who pray in their homes and inviting those in the street to come and pray in the mosque, the minaret came to fulfill the general function of a clock.

Minarets in Cairo were not only attached to Friday (congregational) mosques, but also, as mentioned by the fourteenth-century historian al-Zahiri, to Sufi monasteries (*khanqa*s), colleges (*madrasa*s), Sufi chapels or foundations (*zawiya*s) and even to small oratories. On the other hand one may assume that once it became a tradition to attach a minaret to a religious construction, minarets were built even if they were not quite necessary, for instance in a place already crowded with other minarets. Besides, Cairene architects with their sense for urban architecture and taste for variety must have enjoyed the idea of the minaret forming an additional element to emphasize the facade of their buildings and achieve balance. Minarets must have added status for the sponsor as well as for the architect (al-Mu'ayyad, with its twin minarets, is the only medieval building in Cairo to bear its architect's signature).

Apart from prayer, the minaret is linked to two more of the five pillars of Islam: the duty of "witness" and the duty of fasting during the month of Ramadan. Several times a day it broadcasts the *shahada* to bear witness that "there is no deity but Allah, Muhammad is the Prophet of God"; while in Ramadan, a lantern attached to the top of the minaret used to announce by its extinction that time had come again to start the day's fast.

Travelers' reports and *waqf* (pious endowment) documents confirm that minarets in Egypt were not meant as mere decoration, but were always used by the *mu'adhdhin*. In *waqf* documents the *adhan* called from the minaret is distinguished from the *adhan* called from the *dikka*, the elevated bench inside the mosque. But *mu'adhdhin*s used the minarets for purposes other than the *adhan*. 'Ali Mubarak writes that when an important religious man died, the *mu'adhdhin*s of al-Azhar as well as the other mosques used to repeat certain prayers from the minarets, so that the population would be informed about his death. The historian Ibn Tulun, writing about Syria at the end of the Mamluk period, mentions *takbir*, i.e., calls of *"Allahu akbar"* repeated from the minarets of the mosques by groups of angry people as a sign of protest against the authorities, for example in the case of a man having been unjustly beaten or an official having attacked innocent people, or when sugar was lacking in the markets. Similar protests are reported by al-Jabarti as having taken place at the minarets of al-Azhar.

The foundation deed of the Ottoman amir Ibrahim Agha mentions sums of money endowed by the amir for the *mu'adhdhin*s of the mosque of Qijmas al-Ishaqi so that they would call every morning from the minaret of their mosque prayers to God for the Ottoman sultan, his soldiers, as well as the population of the quarter and for Ibrahim Agha himself. Special recitations during the month of Ramadan also used to take place at the minaret, performed by the *mu'adhdhin*. Royal mosques, such as the mosque of Sultan al-Nasır Muhammad at the Citadel, had up to twenty *mu'adhdhin*s. They performed the royal *adhan* (or *adhan sultani*) in choir. This explains why mosques with more than one minaret were usually royal mosques (with the exception of the mosque of Qusun which is reported to have been adorned at one time with two minarets following an Iranian model). The galleries attached like rings to the minaret were built so that the *mu'adhdhin* could make his call and be heard from all sides. The wooden sticks fixed at the upper bulb were used for hanging lamps, as mentioned in foundation documents.

Three terms are used in Arabic to designate the minaret: the term *ma'dhana*, which indicates its function as the place where the *adhan* takes place; the term *sawma'a*, which occurs mainly in North African and Muslim Spanish terminology and designates a rather squat rectangular structure (though *sawma'a* is also used to designate the hermitage of a monk and in modern Arabic has come to mean

11

silo); the term *manar* or *manara*, which is used in medieval documents and inscriptions to mean the same as *ma'dhana*. It means a place from which light is supplied and is therefore used to designate a lighthouse or watchtower.

Manar is also a figurative term. Maqrizi refers to obelisks as *manar* because of the gold at their apices which reflected the sun's rays. Symbolically, the term *manar* connotes promotion and triumph. To "raise the manar of Islam" thus means to promote it or to achieve its triumph, as in an inscription of the Ayyubid period on the minaret at the shrine of al-Husayn with the name of Abu'l-Qasim al-Sukkari, who sponsored the construction "to please God and raise the *manar* of Islam" (*taqarruban ila allah wa raf an li manar al-islam*). This phrase is also used eulogistically of persons: "may God raise his *manar*" means "may God succor him". The medieval shadowplay entitled "al-Manar" provides an interesting extension of symbolic meaning in the role of the *Manar* or Pharos of Alexandria which is transformed into a fortress that Muslim soldiers have to defend against Christian raids. Such symbolic meanings for the term imply recognition of functions beyond the merely practical, as Ibn Khaldun suggests in a eulogy of the Mamluk sultans when he writes "they erected mosques for prayer and *adhan*... Minarets were raised to ask for forgiveness and for prayer, announcing the tenets of faith".

Essentially a tower, it is no wonder that in many Islamic countries the early minaret borrowed from pre-Islamic tower architecture. Early minarets in Iran, Central Asia and North Africa were similar to previously existing watchtowers: the tower of Qasr al-Hayr al-Sharqi in **Syria** could have been a watchtower or a minaret, or perhaps both; and the towers used by Coptic monks for their retreats in the desert were later turned into minarets. It is probable that such origins never entirely disappeared. Outside urban centers minarets built as such continued to be used as watchtowers as well, as has been suggested, for instance, in the case of the Upper Egyptian Fatimid minarets. The great minaret of the Omayyad mosque at Damascus is reported by Qalqashandi to have been a link in a chain of towers connecting Mesopotamia, Syria and Egypt with a system of fire signals to give the alarm in case of a Mongol attack. The mosque said to have been erected by Ibn Tulun on the site of a pre-Islamic lighthouse on the Muqattam hill likewise had a minaret equipped with a light to guide travellers in the night.

Besides the single lantern hung at the top of a minaret during the month of Ramadan to announce the end of the night and the beginning of a new fast day, minarets used to be, and still are, extensively decorated with lamps both during Ramadan and on other religious occasions. Maqrizi writes for example, that when the minaret of Barquq at al-Azhar was inaugurated, it was covered with lights for the occasion. Dazzled by the lights of medieval Cairo, European travellers gave special mention to minarets. "As soon as the sun goes down," writes Breydenbach during the reign of Qaytbay, "they light many lamps on the towers of their mosques... While watching this spectacle we were struck by the sight of towers sparkling with light, each of them lit with numerous lamps at three levels. Thanks to those lights, the city has the splendor of day". (*Peregrinations,* p. 47.) Another traveler of the same period writes: "An amazing multitude of lamps was burning on top of the towers, so that the city seemed to be on fire; there was also a crowd of priests shouting on the towers. It was like this every night during the month of fasting. The lamps are hung with wooden sticks and lifted with wheels. They carry a small cover so that the wind does not extinguish the flame. Some minarets have forty or sixty lamps and some twenty, according to the endowment made to the mosque. In any case, there were enough lamps on the minarets to give light to the whole quarter during the night. Sometimes at night I would climb on the roof of a house and I would shudder at the ardent fire of the lamps. A Christian with some experience said that no Christian king would ever be able to afford so much money as the fortune spent alone on the oil of the city". (Fabri: *Voyage,* p. 528f.)

The mu'adhdhin

Since the Prophet had a *mu'adhdhin* we know that the office existed before the minaret was introduced into Islamic architecture. The first *mu'adhdhin* of Islam was Bilal, and, according to Arab historians, the first *mu'adhdhin* of Egypt was Abu Muslim al-Muradi, a companion of the Prophet. 'Amr Ibn al 'As, the first Muslim governor of Egypt, appointed for Abu Muslim nine *mu'adhdhin*s for the day and night shifts. Later, Abu Muslim's brother, Sharhabil, became head *mu'adhdhin* at the mosque of 'Amr. Today, though minarets are still built, the importance of the *mu'adhdhin* has greatly diminished; the call to prayer we now hear is often broadcast from a loud-speaker attached to a tape recorder.

According to Islamic law, a *mu'adhdhin* must be an adult, male, pious, trustworthy and educated in law and theology; he must be capable of calculating prayer times, which are set according to the sun—taking place at dawn (*fajr*), at noon (*zuhr*), in the afternoon (*'asr*), at sunset (*maghrib*) and in the evening (*'isha*) — and therefore he must be familiar with elementary astronomy. In this connection it is essential that he be punctual, for which reason he cannot be attached to more than one mosque at the same time. The *mu'adhdhin* is allowed to receive regular pay for the performance of the call to prayer. The four appointed to the Madina mosque by 'Uthman, the third Caliph, were the first to be given salaries. A *mu'adhdhin* could also have a second profession, in which case he was assigned to a mosque in the neighborhood of his work. In monasteries, the *mu'adhdhin* were recruited from the residents of the foundation. Among the perquisites apart from wages, *waqf* deeds mention caps for the *mu'adhdhin*s to keep their heads warm in winter during performance of the *adhan*.

Important mosques usually had their own *miqati,* an astronomer who was appointed especially for the calculation of prayer times and who sometimes acted as the chief *mu'adhdhin.* The *miqati* of al-Azhar in the nineteenth century had six sundials at his disposal, and it was usually from al-Azhar's minarets that the first call for each of the daily prayers would be given, to be followed by all other mosques of the city. In earlier times at Fustat, it was the mosque of 'Amr which fulfilled this function.

Royal mosques in the Mamluk period had a number of *mu'adhdhin*s who, working in shifts, would deliver the call to prayer as a trio from one minaret. We know from Maqrizi that the mosque of al-Nasir at the Citadel had twenty *mu'adhdhin*s and from its *waqf* document that the mosque of Sultan Hasan had thirty. Ibn Battuta relates that there were seventy *mu'adhdhin*s appointed at the Great Mosque of Damascus. Royal palaces also had *mu'adhdhin*s, a practice begun in Egypt with Ibn Tulun, who appointed at his palace twelve Koran readers who were ordered to announce the call to prayer within the palace and to recite glorifications afterward. Ibn Tulun's son, Khumarawayh, famous for his voluptuous style of life, used to make the singers and musicians of the palace interrupt their performances, while he would put his wine glass on the floor, to listen to the call to prayer five times a day. During the Fatimid period the *mu'adhdhin*s of the palace performed their call from within the palace as well as at the palace gates.

Raised up on his minaret, the *mu'adhdhin* is placed in the delicate position of overlooking people's homes, and thus their private lives. Until the nineteenth century, mosques—along with markets—were under the supervision of the *muhtasib,* the man responsible for moral behavior in the city. According to the *muhtasib* manuals, no-one but the *mu'adhdhin* is allowed to ascend the minaret, and then only at times of prayer. He is also required to take an oath, before performing his duties, not to look into the neighboring houses. Historians relate that the *muhtasib* of Kufa, not satisfied with this oath, ordered the *mu'adhdhin* not to ascend minarets except blindfolded. A thirteenth-century lawyer showed similar concern in prescribing that minarets should not be built higher than the surrounding dwellings, or even that they should not be erected in the vicinity of existing houses at all. In practice, a blind *mu'adhdhin* was preferred — an affliction not uncommon in the past. High moral standards were expected of the man's personal life. It is recorded that a *mu'adhdhin* of the *madrasa* of Barsbay at the 'Anbariyyin was severely punished by God for his addiction to liquor, which often led him to call the *adhan* while drunk. During one drunken slumber he dreamt that Sultan Barsbay was beating him on the feet with whips. When he awoke, he saw and felt the evidence of punishment on his body and despite prayers for forgiveness, he remained paralysed until his death.

Plate 1a. The mu'adhdhin

While performing the call to prayer, the *mu'adhdhin* is supposed to face Mecca then turn to the right and to the left. According to foundation deeds of mosques, the *mu'adhdhin* has usually been required to have a good voice. In addition to the *adhan* from the minaret, a second one called the *iqama*, performed inside the mosque just before the Friday prayer, is also part of his work, as well as recitations of religious poetry and liturgical chanting. Mentioning two additional calls to prayer during the night, the first a little after midnight and the second before daybreak, the nineteenth-century writer Lane comments "there is a simple and solemn melody in their chants which is very striking, particularly in the stillness of the night." (*Manners and Customs*, p. 78.) Such additional calls, as well as recitations, chants and the invocation of blessings on the Prophet, are customary during the month of Ramadan.

The *mu'adhdhin* also had the function of carrying out the *tabligh*, which is to repeat what the *imam* preaches on Fridays for those who are too far from the pulpit to hear the preacher properly. Both the *tabligh* and the second *adhan* are usually pronounced from the *dikka* of the mosque, a stone or marble bench supported by columns and standing in the prayer hall. Originally, for example, the mosque of Ibn Tulun had a fountain in the center of its courtyard that was surmounted with a domed structure resting on columns, which was used for the second *adhan*.

The Pharos of Alexandria and the minaret

At the beginning of this century the German scholar Thiersch developed a theory, which he presented brilliantly in a detailed study, based on the fact that the typical Cairene minaret is built in three stories, each with a different section, the first square, the second octagonal, and the third circular. Given the distinctiveness of this feature, he reasoned, the Cairene minaret must have some architectural connection with the Pharos of Alexandria, which was, according to all accounts, constructed in the same pattern. Thiersch collected descriptions of the Pharos in Arabic, Greek, Latin and other European languages, and by comparing the given measurements was able to make a scale-drawing reconstructing it. His theory met with some success until Creswell's arguments pushed it aside; since then Thiersch is no longer seriously mentioned.

According to Creswell's counter-theory, the minaret built in three stories of different sections appeared no earlier than the fourteenth century, by which time the Pharos of Alexandria had already been dilapidated for at least two centuries. The square/octagonal/circular sections of the Cairene minaret, he explains, evolved gradually from the minaret of al-Juyushi to the minaret of Qusun, the octagonal part becoming increasingly elongated until it came to form the entire second story. This evolution supposedly took place without reference to the Pharos.

16

Plate 1b. Instead of a minaret, a balcony is dedicated to the call to prayer over the chapel (*zawiya*) portal of 'Abd al-Rahman Katkhuda at Mugharbilin (1142/1723; *Index* No. 214).

Thiersch's theory, though, is not so far-fetched and still deserves some consideration. One of his arguments is based on the still extant Pharos of Taposiris some twenty kilometers west of Alexandria. Attributed to the Greek period, the Pharos of Taposiris shows the same arrangement as the Pharos of Alexandria: it was built on a square base, grows into an octagon and ends up circular. It is not only depicted in the *Description de l'Egypte,* but can also be seen on a photograph published by Thiersch. Thus the implication is that even if the Pharos of Alexandria was dilapidated by the fourteenth century there was still an extant ancient model for three-stage towers. A further implication is that there may well have been in Egypt an ancient tradition of building towers in three stories, each with a different section, a tradition which could have survived into the Middle Ages. This argument is derived from the fact that in every other Islamic province the minaret usually took its form from towers built in pre-Islamic times. In Iran, for example, the first minarets resembled watch-towers to such a degree that it is sometimes impossible to differentiate between the two; in Syria minarets became rectangular like church towers, and in Iraq, as late as the ninth century the minarets of Samarra looked like Babylonian temple towers. It is quite obvious that local masonic traditions and their approach to the structural problems of tower construction influenced the shape of the minaret.

No traveler to medieval Egypt failed to mention the Pharos, which was in operation until the reign of al-Nasir Muhammad. The Moroccan traveler Ibn Battuta describes it as he saw it on his journey from North Africa to China in the early fourteenth century, noting on his return that it had ceased functioning and that al-Nasir Muhammad had intended to build a new one but had died before realizing his plan. Even if the Pharos had lost its upper story by that time, everyone knew what it originally looked like: "It is needless to describe it," writes 'Abd al-Latif al-Baghdadi in the early thirteenth century, "since everyone knows its appearance". (*Relation,* p. 183.) Maqrizi, who never otherwise gives concrete physical descriptions of buildings, in this case writes a detailed description using material taken from historians and travelers. Ibn Iyas writes that the architect of Sultan al-Ghuri, Mu'allim Hasan Ibn al-Sayyad, made for his master a three-dimensional representation of the city of Alexandria. This model, he says, executed in plaster, showed the city with not only its walls and gates, but also with the Pharos "which used to be there." The memory of the Pharos appears thus to have remained so strong that it continued to be represented as a landmark of the city long after it had disappeared. In a manuscript dated as late as the sixteenth century, the text of an Egyptian shadowplay, entitled "al-Manar" (the Pharos), the Pharos is in fact the main figure, in a plot that deals with Christian raids against the Muslims, the Pharos having now become a pillar of Islam, a fortress which the brave Muslim soldiers defend. It is mentioned as having two stairways; this is also indicated by a thirteenth century Arab historian, Ibn al-Shaikh, who writes that these were in the middle section of the shaft; a feature to be found also on some minarets.

It is not possible today to ascertain with any degree of certainty the extent to which (if at all) the minarets of Cairo were stylistically inspired by the Pharos of Alexandria. Thiersch's idea, nevertheless, is interesting in its own right, and one fact is certain: whatever its origins, the characteristic feature of Cairene (and for that matter Egyptian) minarets is the way their sections change shape from story to story. Even the mosque of Ibn Tulun differs from its Samarra prototype in one important detail: its section changes from square into circular from bottom to top. This change of section-shape can also be seen in the early minarets of Upper Egypt, as well as in the southwestern minaret of al-Hakim, which is strangely missing from Creswell's typology. Built at a time when the Pharos was still intact and functioning, the southwestern minaret is square and octagonal, and the missing original top was probably circular. There are minarets in other regions of the Islamic world, of course, that have square/octagonal or square/round shafts, but in Egypt this pattern is primary.

The stylistic evolution of Cairene minarets

According to Creswell, the minaret of al-Juyushi forms the basic prototype of the classic Cairene minaret which consists of three stories, successively square, octagonal and circular in section. Al-Juyushi's minaret has a rectangular shaft carrying a second, narrower rectangular story with a domed structure on top. It was built in 1085. In the next stage, according to Creswell, the rectangular base of the dome becomes octagonal and the dome develops ribs, as seen in the minaret of Abu'l-Ghadanfar (1157): "The square and circular stories of cube and dome have become elongated and this very elongation becoming more and more pronounced at the expense of the tall square shaft ultimately culminates in a minaret which may be described as having stories successively square, octagonal and square in plan." (*Evolution of the Minaret*, p.10.) The earliest example of the final stage, according to Creswell, is the minaret of Sanjar al-Jawli (1304), whose shaft is of the three-storied square-octagonal-circular type.

Creswell's demonstration of this evolution was mainly aimed at destroying the theory connecting the shape of the classic Cairene minaret with that of the Pharos of Alexandria (see above) by showing that it took centuries to acquire its final shape, long after the Pharos had lost its original appearance. His argument is quite valid if one starts the sequence of evolution with al-Juyushi and ignores the south western minaret of al-Hakim which predates it but has exactly the arrangement Creswell claims to be the culmination of the entire sequence. The south western minaret of al-Hakim (built in 1002) has a square shaft, above which stands a separate octagonal story. Although the original top is missing, one may assume without taking much risk that it was circular, since it was almost certainly domed, the habit of crowning minarets or towers with a domed structure having been established before the time of al-Hakim (Ibn Tulun is reported to have built a dome on top of the Pharos at Alexandria).

In a further development, the octagonal section beneath the dome at the top is transferred to the first level. The earliest examples of this arrangement are the minarets of Bashtak (1336) and Aqbugha (1340). Several minarets are then built with an octagonal first and a circular second story. This evolution leads to the next step: the minaret with both first and second stories octagonal, and the top as usual circular. The earliest existing example of this type is the minaret of al-Maridani. To the square-octagonal and the octagonal-circular, we can add the square-circular composition of Baybars al-Jashankir (1303-4), al-Nasir (1318-35), Faraj Ibn Barquq (1411) and Qanibay al-Sharkasi (1442). There is also the totally circular type represented by Aqsunqur (1347), the western minaret of al-Nasir, and Mahmud al-Kurdi (1395).

The standard Cairene minaret is established by the time of Qaytbay's reign, in the second half of the fifteenth century, while the following reign of Sultan al-Ghuri witnesses the last Mamluk variation on the theme of the minaret: rectangular shafts appear again for the first time since Qalawun, and for the first time since Maridani a change also occurs at the top: the single bulb is replaced by twins, a composition that is doubled again at the minaret of al-Ghuri's complex, which originally carried four bulbs covered with green ceramic tiles.

The addition of stalactites accompanies the development of the Cairene minaret: first (at al-Juyushi) at the top of the square shaft, as a cornice; then below the ribbed helmet; later it becomes the standard pattern at the top of each story, for decorating the transition between two sections. A characteristic feature of Cairene minarets is that no pattern of stalactites is ever used twice on the same minaret: each story is treated differently. A decoration of keel-arched niches filled with a sunrise motif is used on the octagonal sections, whether these form the top story or the first. After the minaret of Qalawun the niches are flanked by colonettes. In the later Mamluk period, more carving is used to decorate the space between the niches and to cover the octagonal section with its columns. Another characteristically Mamluk feature, first occurring on the minaret of al-Maridani and used until the end of the Mamluk period, is the culmination of the minaret in a pavilion of eight slender columns, crowned with stalactites and carrying a pear-shaped bulb. (This gradually replaced the so-called *mabkhara* top characteristic of early minarets, such as Ibn Tulun—a ribbed helmet supported by a circular or octagonal open structure. The minarets of Fatima Khatun and al-Baqli may have acted as transitional stages in this development.)

20

The pierced and carved parapets bordering the galleries of the *mu'adhdhin* have their origins in the magnificent stone screens at the mausoleum of Sanjar al-Jawli. The earliest existing minarets to display this type of parapet are those of Sultan al-Nasir Muhammad at the Citadel. The graceful little balconies we see attached to the octagonal first story of all Mamluk minarets are a combination of this pierced stone parapet and arched panels resting on stalactites. They are purely decorative, and form an integral part of Mamluk minaret style.

The Ottoman conquest of Egypt in 1517 finds its chief architectural expression in the replacement of the Mamluk by the Ottoman minaret in new buildings. Restoration work done in the Ottoman period on Mamluk minarets, while attempting to maintain the original shape, flagrantly attests the decline of architectural craftsmanship during this period. With a few exceptions, it is not until the nineteenth century that beautiful examples of the Ottoman style can be seen in Cairo: the minarets of Muhammad 'Ali, Sulayman Agha al-Silahdar and the one at the shrine of al-Husayn.

Though the Ottoman conquest represents a break in the tradition of Cairene minarets as such, the general architectural tradition and modes of decoration remained faithful to the Mamluks for centuries, despite an obvious decline in craftmanship. The reason why the minaret alone should have changed its style according to political events is difficult to tell. It is a fact, however, that in the history of Cairene architecture there is perhaps no development that can be so closely related to a political change as the transformation of the minaret after the Ottoman conquest. Neither the overthrow of the Fatimid Shi'a rule by the Orthodox Ayyubids, nor the takeover of power from the Ayyubids by the Mamluks caused such a break. Losing its imperial status for the first time since its foundation, Cairo was reduced by the Ottoman conquerors to a mere provincial capital, the residence of a governor, the pasha, in whose career it marked only one brief stage. There is no evidence that regulations were set by the conquerors to subject the minaret to their own fashion, but with a few exceptions all minarets built in Cairo after the Ottoman conquest followed the style of Istanbul. Only in the provinces did minarets continue to be built in the Mamluk style. After his conquest of Egypt, Sultan Selim is reported to have transferred a number of Egyptian artisans and scholars to Istanbul, while at the same time craftsmen from Istanbul were invited to come to Cairo. It was probably during the visit of these Turkish craftsmen that the new minaret style was introduced to Cairo.

It is obvious that Mamluk-style minarets were costly and time-consuming to build, while the Ottoman minarets of Cairo are generally clumsy constructions that must have been easy and cheap to erect. They all look almost identical—a facetted circular shaft with only one gallery for the *mu'adhdhin* and a conical top—and they are usually decorated with a vertical molding running along the

21

facets of the shaft. The transition zone consists of several pyramids rising to the shaft from a base that is mostly below roof-level.

Another explanation of the adoption of the Ottoman fashion and a consequent break with Mamluk tradition may also have been solidity. Mamluk minarets often lost their upper structure: most of the Mamluk tops we see today are modern restorations. An Ottoman minaret presented fewer problems in this respect. There is no need for a staircase to the top, and the upper story, plain and hollow, is much easier to carry.

The minaret in Mamluk architecture had been the structure which, more than any other, displayed the art of stalactite carving: every minaret shaft carried three rings with bunches of stalactites, each differently carved. Beside the minaret, the portal vault and the transitional zone of mausoleum domes were also traditionally decorated with stalactites. The Ottoman conquest had a negative impact on the art of stalactite carving: royal mausoleum domes were no longer built, nor were stalactite portals, which already during the fifteenth century were being partially replaced by portals with a trilobe groin vault. Now, with only one gallery, the minarets displayed only one ring of stalactites. This led of course to a decline in the quality of stalactite carving, which became obvious whenever it was necessary to restore or rebuild a Mamluk minaret in its original style, as can be seen at the northern minaret of Sultan Hasan and that of Ulmas. In their reconstructions of Mamluk minarets, the architects of the Ottoman period avoided the pavilion with the eight columns and set the bulb immediately above the second story. In this context, it is interesting to note that several other Ottoman-period minarets built on pre-existing Mamluk buildings as restorations, demonstrate an attempt to follow somehow the original style, while minarets for new mosques were designed in the Ottoman way. In addition to the minarets of Sultan Hasan and Ulmas, several other Mamluk minarets were replaced by a structure composed of an octagonal first story carrying a cylindrical second story with a conical top. Such, for example, are the minarets of Jawhar al-Lala, Aytimish al-Bajasi, Janibay, or the minaret of Barsbay in the cemetery, which has a retangular first story. This approach to restoration—an attempt to rebuild in a style similar to the original, although its results fall short of the standard of the original—appears for the first time in the Ottoman period. Until then, each restorer had worked in the style of his own period.

The location of minarets

The location of minarets was not a purely esthetic decision for the architect but was governed by a number of requirements which, as the city grew crowded and mosques were built on irregular lots, became more and more difficult to fulfill. A medieval legal text stipulates that a minaret should not occupy a space which could otherwise be used for prayer, and typical Cairo minarets are part of the facade wall, near the entrance, so that there was no real conflict with the prayer-hall. The religious building itself had to be oriented towards Mecca—a requirement which frequently conflicted with street alignment. The entrance portal, moreover, was supposed to lead into the body of the building through a bent entrance, to provide seclusion. Additional structures caused extra problems: when a mausoleum was attached to a religious building, as was often the case, it had to be simultaneously open to the street in order to receive the attention of passers-by, and located next to the prayer-hall to receive the benefit of worshippers' prayers. From the mid-fourteenth century onwards, another important element in the facades of religious buildings gave rise to further constraints: the *sabil-kuttab* (a public fountain with a Koran school for boys, normally located above it). The *kuttab* was supposed to be outside the main body of the mosque in order not to disturb prayer, while ideally the *sabil* should be in a shaded corner, allowing adequate ventilation and fresh, cool water for the maximum number of people.

The location of the minaret, therefore, was often the least of the worries created by this multitude of requirements that the architect had to take into consideration. Among the external elements of religious architecture its location was the most flexible: the only important condition of its design was that it overlook the street, while being tall it could compensate for a disadvantageous location with grace and height. Finally, there was no fixed rule governing the number of minarets attached to one building, (the mosque of 'Amr had five, and al-Azhar six, at one time) and extra ones were often added to important mosques.

The first minarets in Egypt, at the mosque of 'Amr in Fustat, were located at the four corners of the mosque. This arrangement, whatever its origins, had a purpose: it allowed the call to prayer to be heard on all sides above the sounds of a busy port city. The single minaret of Ibn Tulun, however, shows its origins clearly: it is located in the same position as its Samarra prototype—at the northern *ziyada* (close) of the mosque, near its axis. Fatimid minarets seem in general to have been located axially at or over the main entrance of the building. The mosque of al-Qarafa, or the Cemetery, long since disappeared, was reported to have its minaret above the main entrance, as was probably the case with the first minaret of al-Azhar, since the mosque of al-Qarafa was supposedly built on al-Azhar's model. The mosque of al-Juyushi likewise has its minaret located over the entrance. Judging from the buttress on its walls before restoration, the mosque of al-Salih Tala'i, probably did also. The mosque of al-Aqmar was heavily restored in the fourteenth century; it is not possible to trace the location of its original minaret, but the present one, added during the fourteenth century restoration, is located near the entrance and perhaps stands on the original buttress. (The minarets of the mosque of al-Hakim are an exception, in that they

23

project from the corners of the facade wall, a location that may be explained by the essential function of the minaret. Al-Hakim's mosque was built outside the city walls as they stood at that time, before Badr al-Jamali enlarged them. If al-Hakim's architect had erected a single minaret over the entrance in the middle of the western wall, as was common at this period, it would have been too distant from the city. The arrangement of two minarets flanking the facade, i.e. the western wall, placed the southwestern minaret closer to the existing city wall and thus to the eyes and ears of the townsfolk, while the northern minaret, quite remote from the city, could have been used as a watchtower overlooking the caravan road that crossed the northern and northeastern suburbs. An arrangement of four minarets, as in the mosque of 'Amr, would have been functionally superfluous, since the area was not yet urbanized: to the north was the *musalla,* an open ground for congregational prayers on feast days, where there was no need for the *adhan.* Two minarets met the requirement that the call to prayer be heard within the city, provided a watchtower in a crucial position and at the same time presented a balanced composition.)

In the early Mamluk period some minarets, such as that of al-Zahir Baybars, al-Nasir Muhammad's *madrasa,* Baybars al-Jashankir, Amir Husayn and the minarets of Shaikhu, are located above the entrance of the building, like the Ayyubid minaret of al-Salih Najm al-Din. This placement, however, gradually lost favor, and a preference emerged for building the minaret over one of the door jambs rather than directly over the portal vault itself. This preference cannot be explained by structural argument alone, since vaults are in fact an excellent and commonly used method for distributing heavy loads evenly. If most Mamluk minarets are located on one of the door jambs (right or left—there does not seem to have been a preference for one side or the other), it would therefore seem to have been esthetics that led Mamluk architects to this preference—a wish to dramatize the portal. A portal with a minaret built directly above it may not give the impression, when seen from the front, of being adequate either as an entrance or as support for the weight above it and consequently does not stand out as a distinct architectural element. Rarely are minarets attached to the *qibla* (Mecca-oriented) wall, though such is the case with two Mamluk minarets formerly built on the mosque of Ibn Tulun and the Mamluk minaret once added to the mosque of al-Hakim, built probably for dwellers on this side of the mosque. The probable reason why the mosque of al-Nasir Muhammad at the Citadel has a minaret on the eastern corner of the prayer-hall, however, is that at the time of its construction it was bounded on this side by dwellings. The minarets of the *madrasa* of Qadi 'Abd al-Basit and of Yashbak at the shrine of Imam al-Layth are both at the southwestern corner of their buildings, and the minaret of Jaqmaq is located at the northeastern corner of the mosque, while the entrance projects from the southeastern wall.

24

If in early minarets it was symmetry that dictated their placement—on the axis or at the corners—the location of later minarets was dictated by streets. If not located above one of the door jambs, Mamluk minarets could project from any part of the facade and were sometimes not set close to the entrance at all, but were placed so that the minaret could be seen from afar, while the mosque itself, perhaps following the alignment of a winding street, might be somewhat hidden from the passer-by. Descending Bab al-Wazir Street from the Citadel, for example, the minarets of Aqsunqur and Khayrbak seem to dominate the street, attracting and holding one's attention long before their facades come into view, and it is no wonder that these two minarets were particular favorites of the classical illustrators of nineteenth-century Cairo. To a viewer walking south from Bab al-Futuh and Bab al-Nasr, it is the minaret of Qalawun, on the northernmost tip of the complex, that dominates the main avenue of the old city. Further south, the minaret of al-Ghuri, projecting from the southern corner of the facade, gives the illusion that the mosque is closer than it really is, whether seen from south or north, while the minarets of al-Mu'ayyad, with their unique and most prestigious location over the gate of Bab Zuwayla, announce the mosque that can be seen only within the gates. Even in mosques outside the urban core, where space would have allowed symmetry to be achieved if it were wanted, the minaret was erected above or near the opening to the most important street, at a corner (Sultaniyya, Qusun), or on the southwestern wall (Amir Husayn), the symmetry of the twin minarets at the *khanqa* of Faraj Ibn Barquq being an exception. The two minarets of al-Nasir Muhammad, which are not symmetrically located, are placed so as to be best seen and heard from the neighborhood, responding to the same principle.

When a building has more than one facade, the minaret is set at the corner where they meet, so that it can be seen clearly from both streets, as for example at Arghunshah and the mosque of Qaytbay at Qal'at al-Kabsh. In large constructions outside the urban center, like the *khanqa* of Qusun or the mausoleum of Sultaniyya, the minaret was conveniently located at the corner. When such areas started acquiring an urban character in the latter part of the fifteenth century, new minarets took the location they occupied in most buildings within the city—either on the right jamb, as at Qaytbay, or on the left jamb, as at Barsbay. The awkward location of the minaret of Inal is to be explained by the fact that the building was erected in several stages.

In cases where a building stands between two streets, the minaret is located on the more populous side. An interesting example is the minaret at the mosque of Qanibay al-Sharkasi. The entrance of the mosque, in the northern wall, overlooked a square but the minaret stands on the southwestern corner of the mosque, overlooking a side street, where its call could be heard in the more densely populated area. The same explanation applies to the strange placing of

25

the minaret of Qaraqaja al-Hasani, which stands free of the mosque on the northeastern side of the prayer hall, while the entrance to the building is on its axis: the minaret is set closer to the more populous side.

At the mosque of Sultan Hasan, designed to have four minarets, the mausoleum dome is flanked by two, an arrangement unique in Cairo, while two others were supposed to flank the huge portal, an arrangement common in Iranian and Anatolian architecture but never seen in Cairo, except perhaps in the two long-since vanished faience-decorated minarets at the mosque of Qusun, which are reported to have been built after an Iranian prototype.

Most minarets are aligned with the street, following the alignment of the facade, while the rest of the building follows the angle of the Mecca orientation. A few minarets, however, stand at an angle to the street-aligned facade, themselves following the Mecca orientation, an architectural feature that is not quite usual but is exemplified in the minarets of al-Nasir Muhammad's *madrasa* (1304), Ulmas (rebuilt in the eighteenth century), the *madrasa* of Barsbay (1424), Jaqmaq (1449) and Mughulbay Taz (1466). This Mecca-orientation may in some cases have been dictated by structural necessities, the architect making use of a buttress that happened to be part of the Mecca-oriented prayer hall construction, while the street-aligned facade would be a mere screen wall. There is thus no fixed rule for the placement of minarets in late medieval Cairene architecture. The location of each minaret depended on a combination of simple functional requirements and the more complex requirements involved in designing the facades of buildings in an urban context.

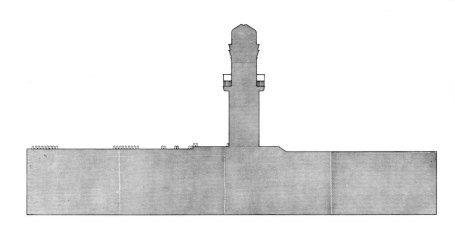

Epigraphy of Cairene minarets

Although not all Cairene minarets bear inscriptions, many do, particularly those from the late Mamluk period.

The first minarets of Egypt, attached to the mosque of 'Amr at Fustat, are reported to have carried the name of their founder, the Omayyad governor of Egypt, Maslama Ibn Mukhallad. The southwestern minaret of al-Hakim also carries the name of the Caliph and a date. Minarets added to existing religious buildings were usually inscribed with the name of their sponsors, so that their contributions would be recorded safely and not overlooked. Thus, the three minarets added to the mosque of al-Azhar by Aqbugha, Qaytbay and al-Ghuri, although they bear no Koranic texts, are inscribed with the names and titles of their founders. The minaret of the Husayn shrine added during the Ayyubid period carries the name of its sponsor, as does that added to the shrine of Imam al-Layth by Yashbak min Mahdi. An inscription band with the sponsor's name has survived from the minaret and pulpit once added to the mosque of al-Aqmar, while the inscription on the minaret of Qalawun was added by his son, al-Nasir Muhammad, after he restored the upper story which had collapsed during the earthquake of 1303—an event also noted in the epigraphy. Apart from these, minarets do not bear foundation inscriptions, which are usually added to the more visible exterior or interior parts of the religious building itself. Most of the inscriptions applied to Cairene minarets are Koranic texts. These may be chosen to suit the construction they adorn: the text carved on the minaret of Qadi 'Abd al-Basit refers to the commandment of pilgrimage, as the building's sponsor was in charge of the veil of the Ka'ba that was dispatched every year from Cairo to Mecca. (Water-fountain epigraphy typically repeats the injunction to provide water to the thirsty; the Nilometer verses refer to water, vegetation and prosperity.) But in general the repertoire of verses applied to Cairene minarets is extremely limited, varying little from the minarets of al-Hakim (the earliest surviving ones to make extensive use of Koranic epigraphy) to those of the reign of Qaytbay. They are usually texts of general meaning, praising Allah as Creator of Heaven and Earth and summoning believers to devote themselves to Him above material rewards. Frequent inscriptions are verses referring to the passage of the hours, night to day, darkness to light: prayer times of course are set according to the position of the sun—dawn, noon, afternoon, sunset and nightfall, and the often-cited Sura III, 190-191 explains the transition from night to day as a sign from God to His believers.

The inscriptions on minarets are not always easy to read, being so high up, and opinions have differed as to whether Islamic epigraphy was intended as communication or as decoration. As far as Cairo is concerned, we believe a distinction should be made between the epigraphy of early and that of later

27

architecture. As early as the ninth century, an interesting document in this matter is provided by the biography of Abu'l-Raddad, the craftsman who carved the inscriptions for the Nilometer of Rawda (Roda Island). He states that he painted the letters in gold on a blue ground *so that the text would be more visible.* (The inscriptions on the Nilometer are legible even today, in fact, without their gold and blue.) Several other examples of early Cairene epigraphy likewise demonstrate, by their legibility, that they were not originally conceived as mere decoration: outstanding instances are the facade of al-Aqmar mosque and the monumental inscription bands on the original minarets of al-Hakim. In fact, most early Mamluk minarets have no inscriptions, which in itself suggests that their architects took epigraphy seriously and meant it to be read. For this reason they preferred to place their inscriptions on more visually-accessible surfaces than minarets, which were too tall and slender to accommodate a legible text.

It is in the late Mamluk period that inscriptions on minarets become most common and are least legible. If we compare the deep carving and large characters of the inscriptions of Qalawun (added 1303), Sanjar (1303) or Tankizbugha (1359) with the inscription bands on the minarets of the Qaytbay period some hundred or more years later, and if we compare as well the location of these inscriptions, it becomes clear that between the fourteenth and fifteenth centuries a change in the conception of architectural epigraphy occurred. The location, as well as the quality, of the earlier carved epigraphy indicate that these texts were written to be read. The same conclusion emerges from a comparison of the carving of inscriptions with that of decorative motifs: in the fourteenth century, the epigraphical carving is executed with more care and depth than the shallow arabesque carving of the same period. Exactly the opposite can be said for the Qaytbay period, the golden age of stone decoration. Here the inscriptions are carved with less care and depth than the rest of the carved architectural decoration. This suggests that the carving of inscriptions had become a routine, and that epigraphy was abandoned to the craftsman in charge of the decoration, who fitted the inscriptions into the composition scheme of his decorative patterns without paying much attention to their legibility. Although it is in this period that inscriptions are applied most extensively—some fifteenth-century minarets carry up to three inscription bands on the first and second stories—the characters are so densely interlaced, as well as being shallowly carved, as to make them difficult to read. The craftsmen of that time presumably did not want to sacrifice the grace of their slender minarets to considerations of legibility which would cause the inscription to dominate the edifice and disturb their decorative scheme.

However, the assumption that inscriptions were originally meant to be read is confirmed by a feature of architectural epigraphy which survived even into the later period, when the inscriptions had become impossible to read. This is the fact that inscription bands are usually oriented, i.e. the *basmala* (opening dedication)

Plate 2 (*right*). The inscription band on the southwestern minaret of al-Hakim (*Photo: Creswell*)

Plate 3 (*below*). The copper boat, or lamp, which used to adorn the domes of Faraj Ibn Barquq (*Islamic Museum in Cairo*)

is visible on the right as one looks up from the street. This would allow a literate person, after identifying the first words, to recall the rest of the Koranic verse even if it was out of sight round the curve of the minaret. (In a few cases the *basmala* begins on the opposite side, i.e. on the right of a person standing at the back of the building. This happened, when the back of the minaret played an important role in its urban setting, as in the cases of Sanjar, Bashtak and Qaraqaja.) It should also be remembered that inscriptions used to be painted. 'As long as the buildings were maintained, their inscriptions were clearer and more visible than they appear today. Besides, for a man on horseback, they were less remote from the eye than they are from today's viewer.

Inscriptions that lost their function as communication, moreover, should not be discounted as mere decoration. They may have had a talismanic value as well, like amulets or expressions of good wishes on objects of daily use. Just as Koran readers were appointed in funeral foundations to read the Koran day and night and to dedicate recitations of certain verses to the soul of the dead buried in the building, so Koranic inscriptions can be understood as a similar ritual gesture. Reaching for the sky, the minaret receives the first and last rays of the sun and announces prayer times to the worshippers. The Prophet is reported to have said in a number of *hadith* that during the call to prayer the doors of the sky are open, and prayers spoken at this time will not be rejected by God. The minaret, with its sacred inscriptions, is a permanent bearer of worship heavenwards.

The finial

Cairo's domes and minarets are characteristically surmounted by brass finials, composed of two brass spheres one above the other, and topped with a crescent, formerly gilt, reminiscent of the lunar calendar upon which Islamic chronology is based.

Despite certain supernatural associations which will be mentioned below, the crescent does not function in Islam as a religious symbol, as does the cross of the Christians, but is used rather as an ornamental sign. It can therefore occur historically in non-religious contexts: in the decoration, for instance, of the boats used for excursion parties on Fatimid feast days, in the adornment of objects of minor art or in jewelery. In the art of the Ottomans, the crescent is frequently coupled with a star, and finials of the same period may take this form, though arrows pointing upward or the word Allah are also not infrequent.

Another kind of finial takes the shape of a boat and is exemplified most notably by the boat that tops the dome of the mausoleum of Imam Shafi'i. The minaret of Ibn Tulun likewise carried a boat-shaped finial from the time of its original construction until last century, when the boat collapsed during a heavy storm. One of the belvederes in the gardens of the Fatimid Caliphs is also reported to have been a dome topped by a boat that, like that of Imam Shafi'i, was filled with grain for the birds. A brass finial from the dome of the mausoleum of

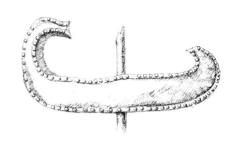

Plate 4 (*below*).   A modern finial

Fig. 1 (*right*).   Boat of Ibn Tulun (*Prisse d'Avennes*)

Barquq in the desert, now in the Islamic Museum of Cairo, carries below the usual crescent a boat-shaped object made of brass with openings that could serve, as in a lamp, for oil and a wick. Although the boats of Ibn Tulun as shown on illustrations, and of Imam Shafi'i both bear a striking resemblance to a certain type of medieval oil lamp,* they are not mentioned as such in the sources, except for the observation that the boat of Ibn Tulun was lit in the Ayyubid period.

Boats appear elsewhere in a context that may be related: provincial shrines used until modern times to include a boat, which on the anniversary of a holy person would be decorated and carried on wheels in a procession. A small boat can still be seen at the shrine of Sidi Sarya, dating from the Fatimid period and rebuilt in the early sixteenth century at the Citadel. A similar boat hangs—inexplicably—on the outside of Bab Zuwayla. The talismanic role of the boat was not restricted to Egypt: the banner sticks of the Saljuks in Iran are reported to have been adorned with a golden boat at their top.** In this context the historian Ibn Tulun provides some information, which although of a later date (early sixteenth century) may shed some light on the matter: he describes two banner poles, one adorned at its top with piece of brass in the shape of a lamp, the other in the shape of the Prophet's slipper.*** In either case—slipper or lamp—the ornament must have looked similar to the boat of Imam Shafi'i, crescent-shaped with one end higher than the other. Boat representations have had a religious function in different cultures from earliest times.

Movement is reported of the finials at both Ibn Tulun and Imam Shafi'i: Maqrizi denies an apparently popular belief that the boat of Ibn Tulun moved according to the sun, and declares that the movement is due to the wind, while on Imam Shafi'i, Lane records a belief that its movements provided good or bad omens. The same belief is mentioned in connection with the crescent atop the shrine of Shaikh Ibrahim al-Dasuqi, which is also supposed to have supplied auguries by its movements. Such supernatural functions may be attributable to the *baraka* (miraculous power) of a saint but also to the crescent itself or to an association with the mosque: even when used in such a non-religious context as jewelery, the crescent is talismanic (it is recorded that even the fall of one of the simple wooden sticks used for hanging lanterns from a minaret at the Citadel was sufficient to predict an accident to the Sultan).

---

*   This resemblance was pointed out to me by Dr. Leonor Fernandes.
**   A. Zeki p. 89.
***   Ibn Tulun uses the term *sanubra* for a certain type of lamp, II, pp. 69 and 75.

The staircase

Most minarets in Cairo have a staircase of their own only above the roof-level of the mosque with which they are associated, although in some instances the shaft of the lower staircase leading to the roof is attached to the minaret so deceptively, the climber may have the illusion that it is contained within the body of the minaret itself. Even such a minaret as that of Qaraqaja al-Hasani, which is located outside and opposite the mosque on a side street, has no lower staircase: it is reached from the roof of the mosque by a wooden bridge at that level across the street. Architects undoubtedly preferred to build their minarets on a solid base, and it is probably for that reason that staircases beginning only at roof-level are the rule.

There are, however, exceptions. When minarets were added to the mosque of 'Amr, for example, they were reached by an outside staircase or ladder and only later, it is said, by a staircase from within the mosque. This peculiarity may be explained by the fact that the original construction of the mosque was so simple that it included no staircase to the roof. When minarets were added they therefore had to be supplied with their own staircase. Later constructions at the mosque of 'Amr included several staircases to the roof and thus to the minarets as well. Another special exception is the minaret of the mosque of Ibn Tulun, where—as in Samarra—the staircase outside the shaft is used as a decorative element; the minaret having thus a solid shaft is, like its Samarra prototypes which survived their mosques, a sturdy construction. The original minarets of the al-Hakim mosque have staircases inside their shafts that begin at ground level, as does that of the small minaret of Abu'l-Ghadanfar. And in the Mamluk period, finally, the rule is violated by the minarets of Manjaq al-Silahdar and Azdumur, both of which are free-standing structures that seem not to have been attached to the walls of their mosques and which carry entire staircases within their shafts.

Except in the case of such minarets, decoration likewise begins at the roof level; this characteristic of Cairene minarets may suggest that the craftsmen who worked on the superstructure of minarets were specialists and were not involved in other structures of the same building.

Four minarets in Cairo have double, parallel stairways, arranged in such a way as to allow two persons to climb without encountering one another: the minarets of Qaytbay and al-Ghuri at al-Azhar and the minarets of Azbak al-Yusufi and Khayrbak. Many minarets in Istanbul have such a double staircase. This feature is less pointless than it seems, since it strengthens the shaft by doubling points of contact between the core and the outer skin. This can also be achieved by diminishing the distance between the flights of steps, as in the case of the minaret of Qusun, where at the middle section the spiral of the staircase is more closely-winding than in the rest of the shaft. The minaret of Sultan

33

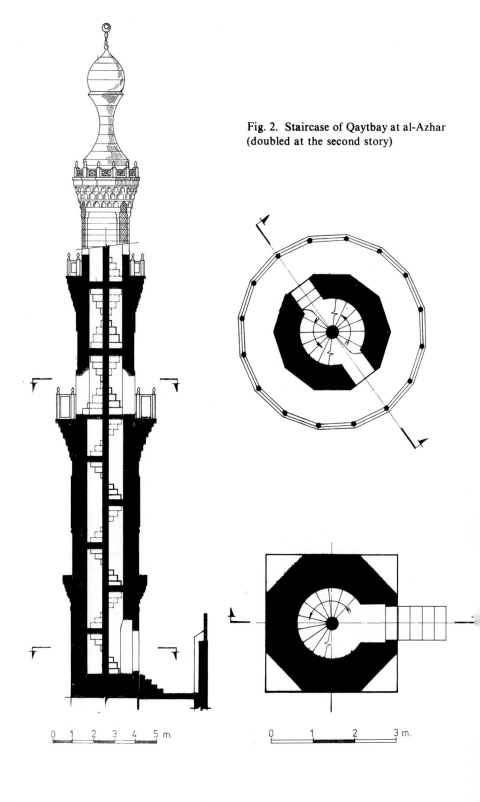

Fig. 2. Staircase of Qaytbay at al-Azhar
(doubled at the second story)

0 1 2 3 4 5 m.

0   1   2   3 m.

Fig. 3 (*left*). Staircase at Qusun, becoming tighter at the middle of the shaft

Fig. 4 (*right*). Staircase at al-Mu'ayyad

Qalawun, though built on a rectangular plan, has a spiral staircase, better adapted to tie the outer skin to the inner core, but the rectangular minarets of al-Salih Najm al-Din and al-Nasir Muhammad at the Coppersmiths have a wooden staircase which runs along the walls of the hollow shaft. Both these minarets are, however, light brick constructions standing above a passage and supported by its side-walls and roof.

The mabkhara and bulb-shaped top

In Arabic the term *mabkhara* means "incense-burner". Its association with an architectural context is modern, originating with the orientalist Richard Burton, who had been told that the Caliph al-Hakim burned incense in his minarets to perfume the mosque. (In fact, it was common to burn incense in mosques since the earliest days of Islam, and of al-Hakim the sources relate only that the pulpit from which he preached on Fridays was adorned with a domed pavilion curtained like a litter, which would be perfumed with incense before his arrival.)

As a specific architectural term, *mabkhara* was introduced by Creswell to designate a type of structure at the top of early minarets consisting of a ribbed helmet supported by an open circular or octagonal structure, such as on the minarets of Abu'l-Ghadanfar, Zawiyat al-Hunud, Ibn Tulun, al-Hakim, Baybars al-Jashankir, Sanjar al-Jawli, Sunqur al-Sa'di, Qusun and Tankizbugha. The *mabkhara* pattern for minaret tops was, however, abandoned during the fourteenth century (its last surviving example is that of Tankizbugha in 1362), and replaced by a structure composed of a pavilion with eight columns crowned by a bulb on stalactites which became the characteristic top of late Mamluk minarets. (The earliest surviving example of such a pavilion is the minaret of al-Maridani; the contemporary minaret of Aqbugha designed by the same architect lost its original top a long time ago. So with few exceptions—the eastern minaret of al-Nasir Muhammad at the Citadel, the minaret of Bashtak (which may have been restored) and the so-called Southern minaret, which did not preserve its original top—the upper stories of all Cairene minarets until the Ottoman period carry an open structure, in the form of either a *mabkhara* or a bulb supported by an eight-columned pavilion.

While the form of the *mabkhara* may be derived from the small dome on the minaret of al-Juyushi (1085) the origins of the bulb supported by columns could be seen as a further development of the *mabkhara*. In this case, the now-missing top of the minaret at the mausoleum of Fatima Khatun (1284), which had a reduced cap carried by a slender octagonal pavilion, may represent a kind of intermediary stage between the *mabkhara* and the bulb. If we assume that the minaret of al-Baqli (1297) is entirely original, moreover, we would see in it the next development, the reduced cap being replaced by a bulbous structure. The

Plate 5 (*left*). An early Christian relief showing the staircase to a monk's hermitage tower (Staatliche Museen Berlin)

Plate 6a (*above right*). A *mabkhara*: al-Salih Najm al-Din

Plate 6b (*right*). The bulb on top of the minaret of Qaytbay in the cemetery

Plate 7. The transitional zone of the minaret of Bashtak and the entrance portal of
the staircase

final development is for the octagonal upper section to be replaced by eight slender columns, presumably to give a more lofty character to the structure.

These slender columns carrying a pear-shaped bulb did not constitute a very sturdy construction: most of the minaret tops in Cairo have either been restored or lack the original upper structure altogether. In the Ottoman period the upper stories of Mamluk minarets were often consolidated by walling up the spaces between the columns, and all the minarets newly built in Cairo during this period are solid to the top.

It has been observed that there is a stylistic relationship between the tops of pulpits and the tops of minarets. The stone bulb carried on columns used on minarets from the mid-fourteenth century onwards, for example, resembles a similar structure found on top of wooden pulpits of the same period, and the conical top of Ottoman minarets also adorns Ottoman pulpits. The description of al-Hakim's pulpit as having a dome carried by an open pavilion extends the traditional similarity back to an earlier period.

The transitional zone of minarets

Like domes, minarets have their transitional zones. The transitional zone of a minaret is the space between the mass of the square base above the roof-level of the mosque on which the minaret rests, and its octagonal first story. The earliest surviving minaret with an octagonal first story, that of Bashtak, is carried on a square base with upper corners cut off so as to form triangles pointing downwards, leaving trapezoid shapes at the four sides just below the octagonal section. These triangles are decorated with a carved undulating motif. Another device is the use of pyramids set at the corners instead of triangles. The transitional zones of the two minarets of Shaikhu at Saliba street show this device and the earlier type: the minaret of the mosque has the pyramids, while that of the monastery is adorned with downward-pointing triangles.

The architecture of this portion of minarets influenced the architecture of domes, which also, of course, have a transitional zone. On early brick domes this zone consisted of steps between the square and the octagonal base of the dome. The development of stone domes, however, led to the adoption of transitional zones similar to those used on stone minarets. The domes of Barquq's mausoleum are thus adorned with an undulating transitional zone like that of Bashtak's minaret. Later domes are also adorned with a molding at their base similar to the molding applied on the base of minarets. There are other examples of the transfer of patterns from minarets to domes: the zig-zag carving which adorns many domes had been used before on minarets (al-Nasir Muhammad, Umm al-Sultan Sha'ban, etc.), while the interlace motif carved on the minaret of Asanbugha has been later used on domes (Umm al-Ashraf, Taghribirdi). The diamond-shaped motif on the minarets of Qadi Yahya at Bulaq and Qaytbay at Qal'at al-Kabsh decorate the mausoleum domes of Qurqumas and 'Asfur. Indeed, the architecture of stone domes themselves, as shown by Christel Kessler, must have been influenced by the techniques tried first on minarets in building *mabkhara* helmets, which were then enlarged to form ribbed stone domes.

*   *   *   *   *

The great majority of the minarets included in this survey belong to the Mamluk period (1250-1517). This is mainly because most of the buildings of historic interest in Cairo were erected by the Mamluks, whose reign had the strongest and most decisive impact on the shape of the old city. Although Cairene architecture had already acquired its individual character under the Fatimids, it is Mamluk architecture that best represents the history of Islamic architecture in Egypt, and characterizes Cairo from medieval times well beyond the reign of the Mamluks, far into the Ottoman period. Modern attempts to revive traditional architecture have always looked back to the Mamluk style, and this is partly because of the great number of buildings surviving from that period, far exceeding those from the previous six centuries of Islamic rule.

Of the period from 641 (the year of the Arab conquest of Egypt) to 969 (the year of the Fatimid conquest), only a few buildings survive, while many great and important monuments have disappeared. Nothing of 'Amr's original mosque remains except our knowledge of its exact location, indicated by the present building. The history of extant Cairene architecture begins, therefore, with the Nilometer and the mosque of Ibn Tulun, both built in the ninth century. As for minarets, these have survived in even smaller numbers than the mosques. From the period between 641 and 1250, the beginning of Mamluk rule, there remain in Cairo only the minarets of Ibn Tulun, al-Hakim, al-Juyushi, Abu'l-Ghadanfar, al-Salih Najm al-Din Ayyub, and a stub at the shrine of al-Husayn: six and a half minarets from six centuries. During these six hundred years Egypt passed through the Caliphs of Madina, the Omayyads, the Abbasids, the Tulunids, the Ikhshidis, the Fatimids and the Ayyubids. The end of the Mamluk period, though it does not imply the end of Islamic architecture in Cairo, marks the end of its golden age. Mamluk architecture in general—and decoration in particular—continued to prevail, but not the Mamluk minaret, which after the Ottoman conquest of Egypt in 1517 was replaced by the pencil-shaped Ottoman one. This development was not, however, accompanied by what Creswell called the "disturbing elements" of earlier periods, but by stagnation: apart from a few minor variations, the evolution of Cairene minarets came to a standstill, and only a selection of Ottoman minarets will be included in this survey.

Survey
of
Cairene Minarets

Note on the arrangement of the survey

The minarets are described in the order of the Chronological Listing which follows. The dates given in this list and in the section-headings are those of the minarets, which may be some years later than the buildings to which they belong. Where two years are given together in the text, the first is the Islamic year, followed by the A.D. year. Where one year only is given this is the A.D. year unless stated otherwise. Index numbers refer to *Index to Mohammedan Monuments,* Cairo: The American University in Cairo Press, 1980.

Plate captions include the date of the minaret in cases where there is no accompanying text.

Transliteration

The Arabic letter *'ain* is represented by ' throughout the book, and *hamza* by ' . Long vowels are shown by bars, and strong consonants by subscript dots, in the Chronological Listing but not elsewhere.

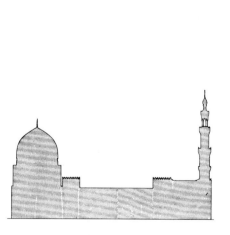

0   5   10 m.

Chronological Listing of Minarets

(Extant minarets built in Cairo up to the end of the Mamluk period —1517—followed by a selection of Ottoman minarets.)

Minaret and *Index* number		Date (A.D.) of minaret	Figure	Plate
'Amr (319)		641		8
Ibn Ṭūlūn (220)		879	1	9-10
Al-Ḥākim bi Amr Allāh (15)		990/1010	5	11-12
al-Juyūshī (304)		1085	6	13
Abū'l-Ghadanfar (3)		1157		14
al-Azhar (97)		various	7	15
al-Ḥusayn, Ayyubid minaret (28)		1237		16
al-Ṣāliḥ Najm al-Dīn Ayyūb (38)		1245	8	17
Zāwiyat al-Hunūd (237)	ca	1250		18
Fāṭima Khātūn (274)		1284		19-20
al-Manṣūr Qalāwūn (43)		1284-5		21
al-Baqlī (156)		1297		22
al-Nāṣir Muḥammad, *madrasa* (44)		1304		23
Sanjar al-Jawlī (221)		1304		24
Baybars al-Jashankīr (32)		1306-10		25
Sunqur al-Sa'dī (Ḥasan Sadaqa) (263)		1315-21		26
al-Nāṣir Muḥammad at the Citadel (143)		1318-35		27
Bashtāk (205)		1336	9	28
Qūṣūn (291)		1337	3,10	29
"Southern" minaret (293)		1340s	11	30
Altinbughā al-Maridānī (120)		1340		31
Aqbughā (97)		1340	12	
Aydumur al-Baḥlawān (22)		1346		32
Aqsunqur (123)		1347	13-14	33-4
Arghunshāh al Isma'ili (253)		1347		35
Manjaq al-Yūsufī (al-Silāḥdār) (138)		1349-50	15	36
Shaikhū, mosque (147)		1349		37
Shaikhū, *khanqa* (152)		1355		37
Sarghitmish (218)		1356	16	38
Sultan Ḥasan (133)		1356	17	39
al-Sulṭāniyya (289)		1360s	18	29
Tatār al-Hijāziyya (36)		1360	19	40
Tankizbughā (85)		1362	20	41

Minaret and *Index* number	Date (A.D.) of minaret	Figure	Plate
Umm al-Sulṭān Shaʻbān (125)	1368-9		42
Asanbughā (185)	1370	21	43
al-Ghannāmiyya, 1st story only (96)	1372-3		
Iljāy al-Yūsufī (131)	1373		44
Barqūq, *madrasa* (187)	1386		45
Maḥmūd al-Kurdī (117)	1395		46
minaret attached to the mosque of al-Aqmar (33)	1397		47
al-Ruwayʻī (55)	1400s		48
Faraj Ibn Barqūq, *khanqa* (149)	1411	22	49
Qānibāy al-Muḥammadī (151)	1413	23	50
al-Zāhid, 1st story only (83)	1415		
al-Muʼayyad Shaikh (190)	1419-20	4,24	51
Qadi ʻAbd al-Bāsit (60)	1420		52
al-Ashraf Barsbāy, *madrasa* (175)	1425		53
Kāfūr al-Zimām, 1st story only (175)	1425		
Jānibak (119)	1426-7		54
Fayrūz (192)	1426-7		55
Taghrībirdī (209)	1440		56
Qānibāy al-Sharkāsī (154)	1442	25	57
Qarāqajā al-Ḥasanī (206)	1442		58
Qadi Yaḥya Zayn al-Dīn, Azhar Str. (182)	1444		59
Qadi Yaḥya Zayn al-Dīn, Būlāq (344)	1448-9		60
Lajīn al-Sayfī, 1st story only (217)	1449		62
Jaqmaq, *madrasa* (180)	1451		63
Īnāl (158)	1451-4		64
Qadi Yaḥya Zayn al-Dīn, Ḥabbāniyya (204)	1452-3		61
minaret attached to the mosque of Amir Husayn (233)	1462	26	65
Sīdī Madyan (82)	1465		66
Mughulbāy Ṭāz (207)	1468		71
Tamīm al-Raṣāfī (227)	1471		72
Timrāz al-Aḥmadī (216)	1472		73
Qāytbāy, mausoleum (99)	1474		6,74-5
Qāytbāy, *madrasa* at Qalʻat al-Kabsh (223)	1475		67
Bardabak (Umm al-Ghulām) (25)	ca 1475		76
Jānim al-Bahlawān (129)	1478		77
Yashbak min Mahdī at Imam al-Lāyth (286)	1479		68
Abu Bakr Muzhir (49)	1479-80		78

Minaret and *Index* number	Date (A.D.) of minaret	Figure	Plate
Qijmas al-Isḥāqī (114)	1481		79
Abu'l-'Ilā (340)	*ca* 1485		80
Khūshqadam al-Aḥmadī (153)	1486		81
al-'Alāyā (348)	late 1400s		82
Qāytbāy at Rawḍa (519)	1491		69
minaret of Qāytbāy at al-Azhar (97)	1494	2,7,27	15
Azbak al-Yūsufī (211)	1495		70
Badr al-Dīn al-Wanā'ī (163)	1496		83
'Alī al-Imarī (426)	late 1400s early 1500s	1500s	84
minaret of al-Ghūrī at al-Azhar (97)	early 1500s	7,28	15
Azdumur (174)	1502	29	85
Qānibāy al-Rammāḥ below the Citadel (rebuilt) (136)	1503		86
al Ghūrī, *madrasa/mausoleum* (148)	1503-4		87
Qānibāy al-Rammāḥ, Nāṣiriyya (254)	1506	30	88
Qurqumās (162)	1506-7	31	89
minaret of al-Ghūrī, 'Arab Yasār (159)	1510		90
Khāyrbak, *madrasa* (248)	1520		91
Sulaymān Pasha (142)	1528		92
Shāhīn al-Khalwatī (212)	1538		93
Maḥmūd Pasha (135)	1568		94
Sīnān Pasha (349)	1571		95
Masīh Pasha (160)	1575		96
Burdaynī (201)	1629	32	97
Ulmās (130)	1713		98
al-Kurdī (610)	1732		99
Abū'l-Dhahab (98)	1774		100
Ḥasan Pasha Ṭāhir (210)	1809		101
Sulaymān Aghā al-Silāḥdār (604)	1837		102
Muḥammad 'Alī (503)	1848		103
al-Ḥusayn's shrine	1873	33	104
al-Rifā'ī	1911		

Lost minarets

A *mabkhara* minaret depicted by Coste			105
The minaret of al-Zāhir Baybars	1269	34	
The minaret in Bāb al-Wazīr			106

46

The mosque of 'Amr 21/641

The first minarets of Egypt belonged to its first mosque, built by the conquering General 'Amr Ibn al'As in his nascent capital of al-Fustat. They were not, however, built at the same time as the mosque itself (641/42), but thirty years later in 673, being added on the order of the Umayyad Caliph in Damascus by Maslama Ibn Mukhallad, his governor, who had his name inscribed on them. At the same time, Maslama ordered that all the other mosques of al-Fustat should be supplied with minarets, so that there should be no further need to use the *naqus*, a sort of wooden bell originally used by the Copts to announce Christian prayer-time.

The four minarets built at the corners of the mosque of 'Amr are called *sawami'* in the sources (plural of *sawma'a*); they were rather simple structures, ascended by means of outside staircases. Their simplicity would confirm the prevailing belief that the original mosque of 'Amr was a rather primitive construction, since it lacked a staircase to the roof. The term *sawma'a* also denotes the tower or column used by early monks for their retreat—its verb *yatasawma'* means "to retreat" and it cannot be excluded that these small minarets with their exterior staircases resembled such hermitages. The mosque of 'Amr was later enlarged several times, decoration was gradually added, interior staircases were built, and in time the roof came into considerable use. It had rooms and other structures built on it and was used, among other things, as an ambulatory, for it was believed that circumambulation there would bring blessings.

The location of the first minarets at the corners of the mosque was interpreted by Creswell as adhering to the arrangement of the minarets of the Great Mosque of Damascus, the capital of the Islamic empire at that time, where the towers of the *temenos* (platform) of an ancient temple, on the site of which the mosque was erected, were used as the bases of the four minarets. This corner location could also have a functional explanation, for each city's great mosque—and 'Amr was al-Fustat's congregational mosque—was expected to provide the initial *adhan* to be taken up by all the others. The mosque of 'Amr was located in the heart of the city, surrounded on three sides by dwellings and bustling market places, and for the call to prayer to be heard at the outlying mosques under such conditions, a minaret on each corner would have been helpful, even necessary. These original minarets must have been replaced when the mosque was enlarged and rebuilt in 709. We know that in the early Middle Ages the mosque had five minarets, two situated at the corners of the prayer hall and three by the opposite (northern) wall.

The minaret at the western corner of the prayer hall, the southeastern corner of the building, was called either 'Arafa or *ghurfa* by medieval historians. ('Arafa is a name; *ghurfa* means "elevated structure" The two words are written identically in Arabic except for the presence of a diacritical dot over the first letter of *ghurfa*.) The tower at the eastern corner of the prayer hall, i.e. the northeastern corner of the building, was called al-Kabira, "the Big One." The northwestern one was called al-

47

Plate 8a. The minaret at the entrance to the Mosque of 'Amr (1800)

Mustajadda, "the Recent One," the southwestern minaret was known as al-Jadida, "the New One". The minaret situated on the northern wall between al-Jadida and al-Mustajadda was called al-Sa'idiyya, probably after the name of an amir of the Fatimid Caliph al-Ma'mun, in whose reign the three minarets, al-Kabira, al-Mustajadda and al-Sa'idiyya, were erected. Historical sources attribute them to his vizir, al-Afdal Shahinshah. As their names indicate, the five minarets were not all built at the same time, nor did they all look alike.

The two minarets we see today at the mosque of 'Amr, one near the main entrance and the other at the southeastern corner, were added by Murad Bey in 1800.

Plate 8b. The minaret at the southwestern corner of the Mosque of 'Amr (1800)

The minaret of Ibn Tulun 265/879

The oldest mosque in Egypt to survive in its original form is the mosque of Ahmad Ibn Tulun, erected in 879 in al-Qata'i', the new capital he built for himself. The second congregational mosque in Egypt, after that of 'Amr at al-Fustat had been the mosque of al 'Askar, the Abbasid foundation northeast of Fustat, but it disappeared centuries ago, and Maqrizi mentions no details relative to its architecture.

The minaret of the mosque of Ibn Tulun is perhaps the most exotic construction in medieval Cairene architecture. It is the only existing minaret in Egypt with a staircase outside the shaft, and for this reason many legends and theories are associated with it. According to one legend, the spiral shape around a truncated cone was invented by Ibn Tulun himself, who is said to have amused himself during a conversation by idly rolling a piece of parchment around his finger. When a bystander sought to embarrass him by asking the meaning of this game, he was not at a loss, but quickly replied that he had been planning the design of the minaret to be attached to his new mosque. The historical sources, however, provide us with a second, less fanciful explanation, which can be confirmed by stylistic comparison. Both the minaret and the mosque itself were built on the pattern of the Great Mosque at Samarra, the Abbasid capital and Ibn Tulun's own place of origin. The minaret of Ibn Tulun is built of stone, however, while the Samarra prototype is of brick, and the plan of its shaft begins as a square before turning circular, rather than following Samarra's continuously conic pattern.

Creswell and other scholars attribute the whole of the present minaret to the restoration work done in 1296 by Sultan Lajin (1296/98), who having once hidden in the mosque while evading enemies, made a vow to restore it if given the opportunity, and on becoming sultan obtained the ways and means to fulfill his vow. Lajin erected the ablution fountain in the courtyard, redecorated the existing prayer niche, built a dome over it and added a second prayer niche. Both the decoration of the present minaret and the octagonal structure, a *mabkhara* on its top, must be attributed to him as well. The arguments of Creswell and others for attribution of the whole minaret to Sultan Lajin may be summarized as follows: the minaret is built in stone while the rest of the mosque is built in brick; both the bridge connecting the minaret with the mosque and the decoration of the minaret, with horseshoe arches and corbels, exemplify an Andalusian style that has to be assigned to the period of Lajin and to Andalusian craftsmen passing through Egypt at the end of the thirteenth and beginning of the fourteenth century as a result of the Spanish Reconquista. Finally, the junction of the bridge and the wall of the mosque — occurring in the middle of a window — likewise shows that the minaret cannot be contemporary with the mosque, but must be of a later date, because if it were contemporary it would have been executed without blocking a window.

50

Plate 9. The minaret of Ibn Tulun

The following counter-arguments can be made: the fact that the minaret is built in stone while the rest of the mosque is in brick does not preclude the minaret's being contemporary with the mosque. Egypt, unlike Mesopotamia, has an ancient tradition of stone architecture, and though the design follows a Mesopotamian pattern, the building of the mosque must have been executed by local craftsmen, who would quite naturally have interpreted the pattern with their native building materials. The traveler al-Muqaddasi, in fact, who traveled in Egypt in the tenth century, reported that the minaret of Ibn Tulun had an outside staircase and was built of stone. The argument of Farid Shafi'i that the stone minaret seen by al-Muqaddasi was a Fatimid construction is too far-fetched, implying that after the minaret of Ibn Tulun had disappeared, it was rebuilt twice on the same model. This implication is quite improbable as judged from all known patterns of restoration and reconstruction in medieval Cairene architecture. Lajin, for example, who built the top of the minaret, the ablution fountain and the dome over the prayer niche in Mamluk style, would, if he had built the entire minaret, have done so in a uniformly Mamluk style. The sources mention Lajin's many restorations but fail to mention any reconstruction of Ibn Tulun's minaret, which is particularly strange in the case of a minaret as prominent and as unique as this one, in a mosque that until the end of the Fatimid period remained one of the major mosques of Egypt, always mentioned by travelers and historians. As has already been pointed out, moreover, minarets added to previous constructions usually bear historic inscriptions. It is therefore a matter of note that the lower part of the minaret of Ibn Tulun bears no inscriptions relating it to Sultan Lajin. Finally, the horseshoe arches and the bridge, which doubtless must be attributed to the period of Lajin, do not necessarily date the entire structure. Neither the horseshoe arches nor the bridge have a structural function, and both could well be part of a later embellishment that included a new stone dressing.

Most probably the minaret was originally not connected to the mosque at all. A story told by the traveller Nasir-i Khusraw, who came to Egypt in the early eleventh century, would seem to confirm this idea: the Fatimid Caliph al-Hakim bi Amr Allah bought the mosque from Ibn Tulun's heirs, who appeared unannounced at the site and began demolishing the minaret. The astonished al-Hakim rushed to the site to demand how they could attempt such a thing after having sold the building. They replied that they had sold the mosque, but not the minaret; and al-Hakim supposedly had to pay an additional sum of money to obtain the minaret as well. (This anecdote recalls the well-known story "Mismar Juha", according to which Juha, after having sold his house, returned every day to a part of it where he had kept all sorts of things hanging from a nail embedded in one of the walls. These daily incursions disturbed the new owners, who protested. Juha answered their protests by saying that while he had sold the house, he had never agreed to sell the nail along with it.) The origin of Nasir-i Khusraw's story may be explained by the minaret's being outside the mosque and not originally attached to the walls by a bridge. Otherwise, it would certainly make less sense!

In his necrologies of the year 743/1343, Ibn Taghribirdi mentions Amir Sayf al-Din Tashtimur, with the usual short account of his life and career. He concludes, as usual, with the amir's construction works, among which he mentions a mosque in the Desert Cemetery and a spiral-shaped minaret (al-ma'dhana al-halazawn), which has not survived. It is not clear from the text if it was a free-standing construction or adjoined Tashtimur's mosque in the Cemetery. But the most striking fact about this information is the description of the minaret as tapering and spiral, the term halazawn in Arabic meaning snail. We may try to guess at its precise form, but there can be little doubt that its architect must have been inspired by the mosque of Ibn Tulun. If this minaret was thought to deserve special attention in the biography of an amir, even though it was not the first example of its kind, then surely the biographers of Lajin, had he been the sponsor of the minaret at the mosque of Ibn Tulun, would not have totally overlooked the fact.

Maqrizi writes that the architect of the mosque was a Christian who had previously built Ibn Tulun's aqueduct and had for some reason been jailed. Upon learning that Ibn Tulun intended to build a grand mosque, the architect offered to design it for him; Ibn Tulun agreed and released him with the commission. On the Friday of the inauguration, as he prepared to pray, Ibn Tulun heard a voice coming from the very top of the minaret. It was the architect, calling for his salary and his freedom! Ibn Tulun gave the man 10,000 dinars and a robe of honor, and he was free for the rest of his life.

At the time the architect climbed to the top of the minaret, it was crowned with a copper finial in the shape of a boat. The boat was still in existence in the nineteenth century, for it is visible in illustrations of the mosque by artists of the period, and served as a model for the one still adorning the top of the dome of Imam Shafi'i. The fact that the tradition of keeping a boat atop the minaret of Ibn Tulun was maintained even after Lajin's restoration is another argument in favor of the idea that the minaret of Ibn Tulun continued to stand, with its boat, until the reign of Lajin, who replaced the boat after the restoration was completed. This means that the original structure never reached such a state of dilapidation that it was necessary to replace it with a completely new one.

In the Fatimid period the Caliph used to pass by the mosque of Ibn Tulun each year in a procession from al-Qahira to Fustat on the day of the Great Festival of the Opening of the Canal, which celebrated the arrival of the Nile flood. On this occasion, we are told, when the Caliph reached the mosque of Ibn Tulun, he was greeted by an acrobat dressed as a cavalier who, perched on top of the minaret, climbed onto a rope attached at one end to the finial and at the other to

Plate 10. The minaret of Ibn Tulun with the copper boat at its top, depicted by Hay

the street and rolled down its length, performing pirouettes until he landed at the Caliph's feet.

Evliya Çelebi, writing in the seventeenth century, observes that the boat of Ibn Tulun had the talismanic function of protecting the city against the dangers of catastrophic Nile floods, talismans being commonly used in medieval architecture on both religious and secular buildings. He also records that an Ottoman amir, excited by the outside staircase of the minaret, amused himself by riding a horse to its top!

Sultan Lajin's addition to the top of the minaret of Ibn Tulun is an octagonal two-storied *mabkhara*. Colonettes can be seen attached to each corner of the octagon below the ribbed helmet. It is the only *mabkhara* to carry this feature and the earliest one made of stone, the next being on the minaret of Qusun (1336). In the fourteenth century, two minarets were added to the corners of the prayer hall by the qadi in charge of the mosque. One of these survived into the beginning of this century but had to be removed because it was no longer securely supported. Judging from an old photograph, it was a nondescript structure of no special interest.

The minarets at the mosque of the Caliph al-Hakim bi Amr Allah 380-401/990-1010

The original minarets at the mosque of al-Hakim are the earliest surviving minarets in the city of Cairo, the older minaret of Ibn Tulun being located in the Tulunid capital of al-Qata'i'. Work on the mosque was started in 990 under al-Hakim's father al-'Aziz; the mosque was inaugurated by him and had been in use for several years before al-Hakim began his own completion works. The southwestern minaret carries the name of al-Hakim and the date 393 (A.D. 1002), indicating that although the mosque had already been in use for more than a decade it had not had a minaret. We know from records and studies of Mamluk architectural practice that it was usual to start the construction of a mosque with the prayer hall, setting the orientation of the whole building. The prayer hall

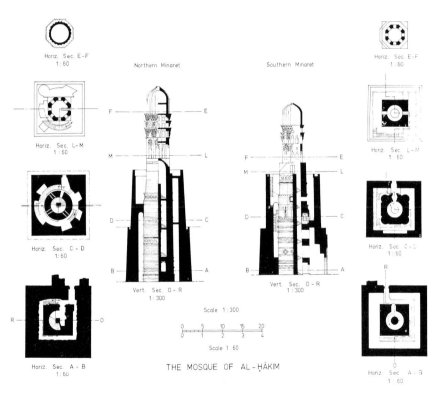

Fig. 5. al-Hakim (*Creswell*)

55

would then be put into use immediately after its construction, before the rest of the mosque had been completed. Nevertheless, it seems strange that a royal mosque would stand for many years without a minaret, unless there was a special reason. If there was one in this case, however, the sources do not mention it.

The two enormous minarets of al-Hakim are attached to the facade wall, projecting at its corners. This location was not an innovation, since the mosque of Amr at Fustat also had minarets at each of its four corners. The surviving portions are built of stone, but their original tops collapsed in the early fourteenth century, and we do not know of what material they were built. Both minarets are structurally independent of the rest of the mosque, and both carry their staircase inside the shaft from ground level so that they do not have to be reached from the roof of the mosque, an arrangement rarely applied in Cairo. Both are decorated from top to bottom, and the decoration is not limited to the facade surfaces but runs around the shafts on all sides without interruption, except where the wall of the mosque once joined the minaret shafts before they were surrounded by the present cubes. Although they are placed symmetrically in relation to the central structure of the mosque, they are totally different in shape and decoration, a fact that led Creswell to assume that they were built by different architects, the one who designed the southwestern minaret being responsible for the design of the similarly decorated portal as well.

The southwestern minaret is composed of a rectangular shaft which carries an octagonal tapering section. At the level where the octagonal shaft begins, there is a small room, very finely carved, which could have been reserved for the *mu'adhdhin* to wait in until it was time to start the call to prayer. This room, which is open to the staircase on one side and to the roof of the mosque on the other, could also have been used as a passage to the roof. Noting similarities, Creswell observes that if the minaret in Sfax in Tunisia is to be dated before that of al-Hakim, its decoration with horizontal bands must have inspired the decoration of this minaret. Since the Fatimids ruled in Tunisia before they conquered Egypt, this would be plausible. It would not be the only example of North African influence on Fatimid architecture in Egypt.

As for the northwestern minaret, it consists of a series of receding cylinders standing on a square base. Seen from the street, however, the minarets of al-Hakim resemble two high towers in the shape of the propylons of an ancient Egyptian temple protruding at either end of the facade wall. Atop each tower, quite unexpectedly, stands a structure in the so-called *mabkhara* style typical of early Mamluk architecture. In 1010, as historic sources tell us, "the minaret was enlarged and buttresses (*arkan*) were added to it". These buttresses were 100 cubits high (about fifty meters or more) and are the cubes we see today hiding the original minarets of al-Hakim within their hollow bodies, to which they are connected with brackets, giving these structures the appearance of flying

Plate 11 (*right*). The northern minaret of al-Hakim with the inscription and the *mabkhara* top added by Baybars al-Jashankir

Plate 12 (*below*). The exterior cubes of the minarets of al-Hakim with the tops added by Baybars al-Jashankir

buttresses, and raising the question of whether they were built because of structural necessity—or because of al-Hakim's many eccentric whims. It is difficult to tell today — particularly when the sources offer no explicit information on this subject — what might have prompted al-Hakim to make such a change. He is described by contemporary historians as insane, and his reign is characterized by abrupt changes of mood marked by a sudden turn towards asceticism. He had already ordered other buildings, for example the mosque of Rashida, to be demolished and rebuilt several times; he also ordered a palace built by his father to be plundered and then demolished. The minarets within the cubes look today like solid sturdy constructions, hardly as if they had once been in such danger of collapse that they had to be supported. If this had been the case, moreover, they would not have survived the violent earthquake of 1303, which destroyed many structures in Cairo, including the upper portions of these same minarets. A change of mood, therefore, seems to be the reason why these great austere cubes wrapping the asymmetrical and elaborately decorated originals were built. Al-Hakim is reported to have started roaming alone on a donkey through the streets of Cairo wearing a plain black woolen garment, his hair hanging on his shoulders, sometimes riding at night in the desert and through the hills watching the stars, and to have practiced magical rites during which he is said to have eaten babies. He could have taken a sudden dislike to the minarets and ordered new ones with a symmetrical and more severe outlook to be built in their stead. The architect, not willing to destroy the originals, masterpieces of architecture and stone carving, enveloped them in the cubes, but in such a way that they still can be seen inside. It is also possible that the original minarets had already been started by his father al-'Aziz and were merely completed by al-Hakim — hence his name and the date on the southwestern shaft — who then disliked them and had them replaced by structures to his own taste.

The southwestern cube is adorned with finely carved Koranic texts differing from those on the interior shaft. At the roof level the remains of a crenellation can be seen that resemble the intricate crenellation of the mosque of Ibn Tulun, which also inspired the building's arcades. This is the only surviving example showing an attempt to imitate Ibn Tulun's crenellation. The remaining crenellation of the mosque is of the usual stepped type and may be due to a later restoration, since the building was severely damaged by the earthquake of 1303 and had to be largely rebuilt. The top of the southwestern cube is decorated with a stucco band carrying an interlace pattern frequently used on Fatimid prayer niches. As for the northwestern cube, its lower part was incorporated into the masonry of the city walls when they were enlarged by Badr al-Jamali almost a century later, al-Hakim having built his mosque outside the old walls. The upper part of the northern cube carries a Koranic stucco inscription, which starts on the eastern side of the cube. The fact that the text of the inscriptions begins on the eastern side of the minaret, facing Bab al-Futuh near which the minaret stands, can perhaps be explained by the processional route that traditionally passed through Bab al-Nasr and not Bab al-Futuh. This inscription, in Mamluk *naskhi* cript, must have been added by Baybars al-Jashankir.

The earthquake of 1303 took place during the reign of al-Nasir Muhammad who charged each of his amirs with the restoration of a damaged building. Baybars al-Jashankir was assigned the minarets of al-Hakim. He added the two *mabkhara* tops built of brick, each composed of a ribbed helmet above an octagon decorated with stalactites. With different arrangements in the octagonal sections, the two structures are not identical. During this restoration, a small box was reportedly found within the walls of the northwestern minaret adjoining Bab al-Futuh, which upon being opened, revealed a human hand wrapped in cotton and carrying an indecipherable inscription. The hand looked, it is said, as fresh as if it just been cut off.

In 1423, a merchant added one more minaret to the mosque of al-Hakim, at the southeastern wall near the prayer niche, but this one has since disappeared.

The minaret of al-Juyushi 478/1085

The mosque of al-Juyushi on the Muqattam hill, built by the vizir Badr al-Jamali, who also built the walls of Cairo, has a minaret said to have been inspired by North African architecture. It is built on the same pattern as the minaret of Qayrawan, erected in the ninth century, and consists of a rectangular shaft carrying a second, narrower rectangular story with a domed structure on top. The domed structure is built in the same style as the dome above the prayer hall. At the top of its shaft the minaret of al-Juyushi carries the earliest stalactites in Cairene architecture.

The name of the mosque derives from Badr al-Jamali's title as commander of the army — *amir al-juyush* — and an interesting theory attributes the whole building to a purpose other than religious or funerary: it is interpreted by Farid Shafi'i as a military watch-tower "disguised as a mausoleum." According to Shafi'i, the minaret of al-Juyushi, being equally visible from most parts of Cairo, could conveniently have been used to give light signals, to observe suspicious gatherings of people in any part of the city or to warn of the advance of troops coming from Upper Egypt, where Badr al-Jamali succeeded in subduing rebellions. In this period Egypt was also threatened by a possible attack from Sunni antagonists abroad, which explains his care to renew the city's fortifications. "It is difficult to believe that the site on which the monument was built had once been so crowded with people occupying high buildings that calling them to prayer required a high massive minaret," writes Farid Shafi'i. One could apply the same words, however, to many of the minarets connected to tombs in the cemeteries of Cairo, most of which, according to this argument, would have no real justification for standing where they are. The mosque of al-Juyushi has on its roof small domed structures that look like little kiosks, large enough to allow one person to stand inside. Within each of these structures is a small prayer niche. If the domed structures were meant as shelter for the guards, as suggested by Shafi'i, these prayer niches would have no justification, since the Mecca orientation is given by the orientation of the prayer hall anyway and is, moreover, enhanced by the presence of a dome over the main prayer niche. Most probably the small domed structures were cells for the retreat of Sufis for prayer and meditation (*khalwa*). In this case the mosque of al-Juyushi was erected primarily as a religious building, though such a conclusion does not preclude its having had a military function at the same time.

Plate 13. The mosque of al-Juyushi

Fig. 6. al-Juyushi

Plate 14. The minaret of Abu'l-Ghadanfar

The minaret of Abu'l-Ghadanfar 552/1157

This minaret is the only surviving structure of the original building. It may not be impressive, but it is the earliest existing minaret of the *mabkhara* type — a square shaft that carries an octagonal two-storied structure surmounted with a ribbed helmet (see section on *mabkhara*). Below this helmet the octagonal structure is pierced on all sides with lobed openings. Abu'l-Ghadanfar's *mabkhara* lacks the stalactites to be seen on later minarets of the same type, but these may simply have fallen off since the minaret is built in brick covered with plaster. The staircase starts at ground level.

61

The minarets of al-Azhar

The mosque of al-Azhar has been one of the world's primary institutions for the teaching of Islamic theology since the early Middle Ages. No wonder that so many constructions were regularly added to it, enlargements and adjoining *madrasa*s as well as minarets. Minarets at al-Azhar have come and gone, but unfortunately no minaret of the Fatimid period has survived: during the reign of Sultan al-Zahir Baybars (1260-77), consensus had it that the existing minaret was too short, so an upper structure was added to it, but it was still too short for Barquq's taste (1382-99), so in 1397 he decided to tear down the whole minaret and build a new one. Maqrizi informs us that to support this new structure a vault was built at the northern entrance, with stones taken from the *madrasa* of al-Ashraf Khalil at the Citadel, which Barquq had demolished. This information seems to indicate that the previous minaret had also been located at the northern entrance. Barquq lived to see the completion of his minaret at al-Azhar, but not its collapse some twenty years later. It was rebuilt by al-Mu'ayyad Shaikh (1412-21), but had to be demolished soon after its completion in 1423 due to a similar structural deficiency. The oldest surviving minaret at al-Azhar is the minaret attached to the *madrasa* of Aqbugha, built in 1339. One wonders how Maqrizi, our primary source for the Mamluk history of Cairo and its architecture, could state that the minaret of Aqbugha was the second minaret to be built in stone after that of Qalawun, thus overlooking al-Hakim (1010), Fatima Khatun (1284), Sanjar (1304) and Bashtak (1335). Even if the minaret of Ibn Tulun is attributed to Lajin, it would also be earlier (1296). Perhaps Maqrizi meant that it was the first to be built totally in stone, since of all these earlier minarets, Ibn Tulun is the only one certain to have been completely built in stone: the stone upper structure at the minaret of Bashtak may be due to restoration in the Ottoman period, and all other earlier examples have a brick upper structure.

Maqrizi writes that the *madrasa* of Aqbugha was a depressing place. It lacked the usual flavor of places of worship, he notes, because the land it was built on was acquired illegally and the workers were abused and ill-treated during its construction. Despite this unfavorable beginning its minaret has survived, perhaps because it was designed by the talented royal chief architect, Mu'allim al-Suyufi. His original minaret stops at the level of the second inscription band. The bulb at the top, part of a recent restoration, is most probably inauthentic: judging by contemporary examples, and especially by the minaret of al-Maridani designed by the same architect, a third story is missing, which may have been either a bulb carried by columns, as in the case of al-Maridani, or perhaps a *mabkhara*. Whatever its pattern, a third story must have existed, with the open structure common to all Mamluk minarets.

62

Plate 15. The minarets of al-Azhar; from left to right: Qaytbay, Aqbugha, al-Ghuri

The minaret added to al-Azhar by Qaytbay, probably in 1494, located on the right side of the portal also added by him, is a masterpiece of stone carving, so superlative in workmanship that it was impossible for the craftsmen of al-Ghuri, who built the next minaret attached to al-Azhar, to surpass it. The architect entrusted with al-Ghuri's minaret therefore emphasized originality of design and the sheer height of his minaret, creating a structure that is octagonal at the first story and facetted at the second, with decoration composed of inlaid ceramic tiles forming arrow motifs as well as inscriptions. The upper story of al-Ghuri's minaret is double-headed, like the two minarets of Qanibay al-Rammah built in the same period (early 1500s), and has a double staircase at the level of the second story, allowing two persons to climb up the minaret at the same time without seeing each other, a device also used in the al-Azhar minaret of Qaytbay, as well as in the slender minaret of Azbak al-Yusufi (1495) and that of Khayrbak (1520). The double-headed minaret has also been used at the mosque of Janbalat (who ruled for only one year, 1500-1501), whose two stone domes and double headed minaret were visible until the French destroyed the entire building for strategic reasons three centuries later.

In addition to the inscription bands with the names and titles of the Sultan al-Ghuri, his minaret carries one badly-preserved inscription at the lower part of its northern side with the title of *amir akhur* (amir in charge of the royal stables) and a name which could be identified as al-Mujibi Aldumur, probably an amir in charge of the construction of the minaret.

In the eighteenth century 'Abd al-Rahman Katkhuda, who restored a large number of Cairene monuments, added three minarets to the mosque of al-Azhar. Two of them survive on the southern and southeastern walls, both unpretentious constructions in the Ottoman style.

The minarets of al-Azhar have witnessed some events worth mentioning, since they underline the uses to which minarets may be put. In the sixteenth century, for example, one of the governors of Egypt, Iskandar Sharkas, who turned out to be a tyrant and despot of such proportions that the Ottoman sultan himself felt obliged to recall him to Istanbul, was publicly cursed from the minarets of al-Azhar. In 1785, when the beggars who received their daily bread from the pious foundations attached to al-Azhar found this charity suddenly cut off, they closed the doors of the mosque (thereby preventing prayer), climbed the minarets and shouted their claims into the city of Cairo, repeating their demonstrations several times until the promise to restore their bread was in fact fulfilled. Hearing about the success of their method, groups from the popular quarter of Husayniyya marched to al-Azhar in the same year, armed with sticks and pounding drums, and likewise climbed the minarets for maximum audibility and visibility.

Fig. 7. Qaytbay (left) and al-Ghuri at al-Azhar

Plate 16. The Ayyubid stub at the
shrine of al-Husayn

Even Napoleon made use of al-Azhar as a publicity center when, having
conquered the city of al-'Arish in Sinai, he celebrated his triumph by raising two
flags captured from the enemy over the double-headed minaret of al-Ghuri.
Cannons were fired to enhance the festivities. Later, after the conquest of Yaffa,
he restricted his victory proclamation to hanging captured banners at the doors of
the mosque.

The Ayyubid minaret at the shrine of al-Husayn 634/1237

Only one and a half minarets have survived from the Ayyubid dynasty which ruled
Egypt after Salah al-Din overthrew the Fatimids (1171-1250). The complete
surviving minaret is described in the next section. The half is at the venerated
shrine of al-Husayn, established under the Fatimids within the confines of the
Great Palace. It stands over a passage known as al-Bab al-Akhdar, a square shaft
without its original top, all that has survived of a minaret sponsored in 1237 by a
man named Abu'l-Qasim al-Sukkari, as stated in an inscription slab. The shaft is
decorated with three panels of most finely carved pierced stucco resembling lace
and having medallions. The passage (which probably dates from the Fatimid
period) and the minaret above it, are the only ancient structures to have been
preserved at the shrine. The upper part of the minaret is an eighteenth-century
addition by 'Abd al-Rahman Katkhuda.

66

Plate 17. The minaret of al-Salih
Najm al-Din Ayyub with a *mabkhara*
top

The minaret of al-Salih Najm al-Din Ayyub 641/1245

Only one complete minaret of the Ayyubid period has in fact survived. It is
known as the minaret of al-Salih Najm al-Din, the last of the Ayyubid sultans.

According to the Shafi'i rite to which the Ayyubids adhered, only one
congregational, or Friday mosque is allowed within each urban agglomeration.
The mosques of 'Amr at Fustat and al-Hakim in al-Qahira satisfied this
requirement. The Ayyubids therefore did not build Friday mosques in Fustat or
Qahira, but they did build a number of *madrasa*s adorned with minarets where the
five daily prayers were announced. Evliya Čelebi writes in the seventeenth century
that the *madrasa* of the Ayyubid Sultan al-Malik al-Kamil had a minaret and a
dome attached to it, their location being the same as at the *madrasa* of the
Mamluk Sultan Barquq next door, but their architecture being different. Since
both dome and minaret of the Ayyubid *madrasa* no longer exist, it cannot be
stated whether what Evliya Čelebi saw was an original part of the building or a
later addition. The distinction he draws, however, between, the shape of this
minaret and the minaret of the Mamluk *madrasa* may suggest that the former was
a minaret of the Ayyubid period.

67

1 : 50

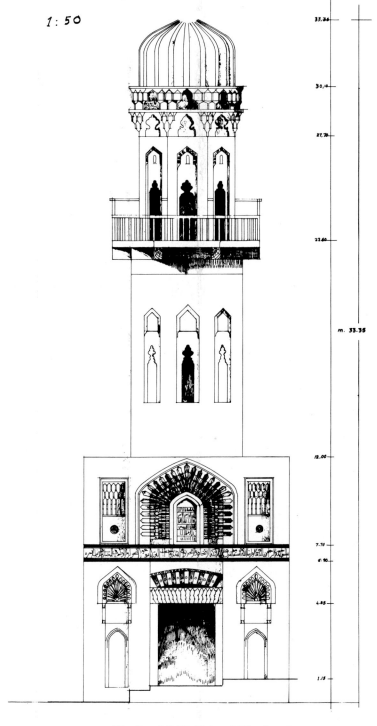

Fig. 8. al-Salih Najm al-Din Ayyub

Plate 18. The minaret of Zawiyat al-Hunud with a *mabkhara* top (*ca*1250)

The minaret of the *madrasa* of al-Salih Najm al-Din, built on the site of the Great Palace of the Fatimid Caliphs in the heart of the capital, is the earliest surviving minaret of the *mabkhara* type after that of Abu'l-Ghadanfar, and the third royal minaret after those of Ibn Tulun and al-Hakim. It stands over a passage between the two wings of the college and had access from the wooden roof of this passage, which has since disappeared. The minaret itself is a square shaft carrying an octagonal second story pierced on each side with keel-arched niches. Two rows of stalactites decorate the octagonal story, which itself supports a ribbed helmet. A wooden balcony runs around the space between the square shaft and the octagonal section. The shaft itself is decorated with keel-arched niches carved with stucco panels bearing the typical Fatimid radiating motif, which have survived on the inward face of the minaret but have perished on the streetward side. The whole minaret is built in brick with a wooden staircase.

The minaret of al-Salih, with its stalactite cornice beneath the *mabkhara* helmet and keel-arch decoration on the facets of the octagonal second story, is the earliest example to show this combination, thus representing the standard pattern for all later minarets of the *mabkhara* type.

69

The minaret of Fatima Khatun 683/1284

Only a massive rectangular shaft has survived from the minaret of Fatima Khatun, located on the left side of the entrance to the *madrasa,* but luckily two old photographs can still testify to the original appearance of the minaret, showing that its square shaft, very similar to that of Sultan Qalawun, once carried a slender open polygonal structure crowned by a small cap. The surviving shaft is in stone, while as the photograph shows, the missing top was built in brick. This minaret was thus built in two stories. The cap at the top was smaller than is usual in surviving *mabkhara* minarets. It is possible that this reduced cap was an intermediary stage between the *mabkhara* helmet and the bulb used later on the classic Cairene minaret.

The minaret of Sultan al-Mansur Qalawun 684/1284-5

Like many other features of the Qalawun complex, its minaret seems to emerge suddenly into the architecture of Cairo without stylistic precedent either in the city or elsewhere. Some elements of the arrangement of the minaret of Qalawun recall the arrangement of the minaret of al-Juyushi: it is rectangular, built in three stories, with the upper level receding. The scale, however, is completely different, and except for the minarets of al-Hakim, its massiveness is unparalleled in Cairene architecture. Nor does its architecture seem to have a foreign prototype, though the rest of the Qalawun complex has been compared with Norman-Sicilian and Byzantine architecture. Unlike previous Cairene minarets, such as al-Juyushi, al-Salih and al-Zahir Baybars, the minaret of Qalawun is set at a distance from the entrance. It stands on the northern corner of the building with the mausoleum dome and the rest of the complex to its rear. From this exposed position it faces Bab al-Nasr and Bab al-Futuh, the starting point for the post-investiture processions of the sultans through the city to the Citadel. The tradition of these processions, which began with Salah al-Din, ended after the death of Sultan al-Nasir Muhammad in 1341. The inscriptions of the minaret start on the northern side, facing the procession road.

The decoration of Qalawun's minaret, like that of Ibn Tulun, includes horseshoe arches and double windows, features typical of Andalusian architecture, which can be explained by the presence in Egypt of Andalusian craftsmen who were no longer able to practice their skills in Spain and so had gone to Cairo, where the building activity was intense at this time. The minaret of Qalawun is the first to bear an element which became an integral part of Cairene minaret decoration from then on: the arched panel on each face of the minaret, flanked by colonettes and resting on a stalactite. The third story, unlike the rest of the shaft, is decorated with lacy stucco carving, similar to the stucco on the minaret of the *madrasa* of Qalawun's son, al-Nasir Muhammad, next door. This

70

Plate 19 *(above left)*. The minaret of Fatima Khatun photographed last century with its original top in the shape of a reduced *mabkara*

Plate 20 *(below left)*. The truncated minaret of Fatima Khatun today

Plate 21 *(right)*. The minaret of al-Mansur Qalawun with the third story added by his son al-Nasir and the cap at the top added in the Ottoman period (note the lamp sticks)

Plate 22. The minaret of al-Baqli

stucco is in fact al-Nasir's addition to his father's minaret after the damage caused by the earthquake of 1303. The inscription of Qalawun's minaret bears al-Nasir's name and commemorates the earthquake and subsequent restorations. The upper cornice of this third story has been compared by Creswell to an ancient Egyptian reed motif and appears later in the minarets of Shaikhu and Manjaq. The ugly cap crowning the upper cylinder is an Ottoman contribution.

In the year 1425, a tightrope walker stretched a rope from the finial of Qalawun's minaret to that of Barquq's, then suspended a second rope from its mid-point, thrilling a crowd by climbing up and down, walking back and forth and performing all kinds of fantastic capers.

The minaret of al-Baqli ca697/1297

Although a modest construction, this minaret presents an item of archeological interest. Its square shaft is of the Fatima Khatun type as is the slender octagonal structure above it and the double molding which crowns it. The two minarets are in fact almost identical, with the exception that instead of the reduced *mabkhara* in the shape of a small helmet, a bulbous structure can be seen at the top. If this bulbous structure is original, it would be the earliest known example of its type,

72

coming long before the bulb on the top of al-Maridani's (1334) or al-Nasir's minarets at the Citadel (1318-1335). A document that seems to support the idea that this top is original is the illustration in the *Description de l'Egypte* of a nearly identical minaret from the eastern cemetery (no longer extant), suggesting that there existed a type of minaret composed of a square shaft carrying an octagon with a bulbous top instead of a *mabkhara* helmet, of which al-Baqli is the only surviving example (see chapter on stylistic evolution).

The minaret at the madrasa of Sultan al-Nasir Muhammad 703/1304

The facade of the *madrasa* of Sultan al-Nasir Muhammad suffers from a most disadvantageous location. From the south it is hidden behind the corner of Qalawun's complex and dominated by its massive minaret. Seen from the north, it is squeezed between the *madrasa* of Sultan Barquq and the minaret of Qalawun, and in fact the famous Gothic portal, composed of spoils from the Crusaders and praised by Maqrizi as one of the most magnificent in the world, cannot be seen until one stands right in front of it.

The square shaft is built in brick and is light enough to be carried by the two walls that form the passage between the college on the southern and the mausoleum on the northern side of the building. The filigree-like decoration of the shaft, all in stucco, perhaps too delicate for its body, is composed of keel-arched panels, diamond shapes, medallions, and an inscription band with the name and title of the Sultan. The decoration on the back side of the minaret has totally disappeared. The inscription band starts on the northern side of the minaret but, like the rest of the stucco decoration on this side, does not cover the whole wall, thus leaving undecorated a space over the whole length of the first story near the western corner of the minaret. Why was this space left plain? In order to understand the difficulty confronting the craftsman at work, we must remember that there was a mausoleum dome, which today does not exist, close to the northwestern corner of the minaret, almost touching it, as the surviving base of the dome indicates. By the time the construction of the dome was terminated, it had hidden and blocked this corner of the minaret, which would not be decorated until after the completion of the dome. The craftsman in charge of the decoration was thus obliged not only to leave this portion undecorated, but also to start the inscription at a point where he had enough room to stand and work. Had he started the inscription on the portal side (i.e., the eastern side) as was usual on minarets of the same period, the inscription on the northern band would have been interrupted at the point where minaret and dome met. Only by starting the inscription on the northern side of the minaret could he complete the text before it

Plate 23. The minaret at the *madrasa* of al-Nasir Muhammad (the second story is probably not original)

reached the dome on the back side. It is clear that in medieval Cairo, buildings were not always planned beforehand to the last detail.

The staircase of this minaret is not of the usual spiral type, but runs around a square space inside the body and is made of wood, as is the staircase of the minaret of al-Salih, perhaps to keep the minaret light as it does not rest on a buttress. The octagonal second story does not seem to be an original part of the minaret and is probably an addition of the fifteenth century. The structure at the top dates from the Ottoman period. The minaret of al-Nasir Muhammad does not follow the line of the facade of the *madrasa* but forms a slight angle to it, thus more accurately following the Mecca orientation. This deviation does not necessarily imply a religious motive, but may have had a structural reason, due to the orientation of the walls carrying the minaret.

The minaret at the mausoleum of Sanjar al-Jawli 703/1304

What is most remarkable about the *madrasa* and double mausoleum of the two friends, Salar and Sanjar al-Jawli, is its extraordinary front elevation, composed of a minaret standing next to two unequal domes, all atop a handsome building perched on a rocky cliff that dominates the view from the Citadel along Saliba Street, one of the processional roads of medieval Cairo. At the time it was erected, the quarter of Qal'at al-Kabsh behind it had a residential character and

Plate 24. The minaret of Sanjar
al-Jawli

Sanjar himself had his palace there, which explains the presence on this side of a handsome stalactite portal leading to the funeral complex through a passage.

The minaret is composed of a rectangular stone shaft with a two-storied brick *mabkhara* structure. The rectangular part follows stylistically the tradition of Qalawun's minaret — each face of the shaft is adorned with arched panels flanked with colonettes and resting on stalactites; there are bull's eyes and cushion *voussoirs* as well. The octagonal base of the *mabkhara* here forms a distinct elongated second story which, with the third story of circular section, is the earliest surviving example of three-storied square-octagonal-circular composition which will become the standard form of Mamluk minarets. (From the second story upwards it is built in brick.) An unusual feature, which can be explained by the desire of the architect to add esthetic elements to the side of the building overlooking Qal'at al-Kabsh, is that the entrance to its staircase, at roof level, has a trilobe portal like that of an independent building.

The intention of the architect to address viewers on both sides of the building is indicated as well by the arrangement of the Koranic inscription bands which adorn it: while the inscription on the minaret begins facing Saliba Street, thus reflecting the more public function of the minaret, the inscription on the funeral domes begins facing the quarter of Qal'at al-Kabsh.

The minaret of Baybars al-Jashankir 706-9/1306-10

This minaret displays an arrangement which has no parallel among the extant minarets of Cairo: it has a *mabkhara* top carried by a circular section resting on a rectangular shaft. Usually the *mabkhara* is carried by an octagonal second story. A photograph taken last century by Frith, however, shows another minaret very similar to that of Baybars al-Jashankir (see section on lost minarets), the only difference being that the helmet rests immediately above the cylindrical section without the intermediate pierced pavillion. The rectangular shaft of Baybars' minaret is crowned by bunches of stalactites recalling those at the minaret of al-Nasir's *madrasa*. The ribbed helmet of the *mabkhara* was once covered with green tiles, of which only traces are visible today.

Baybars al-Jashankir built his monastery (*khanqa*) first, then added the mausoleum dome and the minaret. The foundation deed (*waqf*) of the complex was written before the dome and the minaret were erected. It states that a minaret

76

Plate 25. The *mabkhara* minaret of Baybars al-Jashankir

should be added at an adequate location, without specifying which. It was placed above the portal, receding from the facade.   In spite of the difficulties which confronted the architect while adding a dome and a minaret to the facade, both structures make a particularly harmonious picture.

The minaret of Sunqur al-Sa'di (Hasan Sadaqa) 715-721/1315-21

This minaret is decorated below the *mabkhara* helmet with a cascade of stalactites on two stories which, combined with the slender elongation of the shaft, creates an unusual effect. The finial is not the usual copper crescent, but represents the cap of an Ottoman Mawlawi Derwish; in fact the building, originally a *madrasa* and *ribat* for women (a kind of asylum), was used as a convent for the Sufis of the Mawlawi order from the Ottoman period onward.

The minarets of Sultan al-Nasir Muhammad at the Citadel 718-735/1318-35

The exotic minarets of the royal mosque of Sultan al-Nasir Muhammad at the Citadel, the residence of the sultans, and particularly their garlic-shaped crowns covered with faience mosaics, record an event of special interest, the arrival in Cairo of a craftsman from Tabriz. Sultan al-Nasir Muhammad had established friendly diplomatic relations with the Mongol court of Iran and was married to a Mongol princess.   One result of this entente was that when the Mamluk ambassador to the court of Abu Sa'id returned to Egypt, he brought with him a craftsman who is said to have built two minarets for the mosque of Amir Qusun on the pattern of the minarets of the mosque of 'Ali Shah at Tabriz. Unfortunately, neither the minarets of 'Ali Shah nor those of Qusun have survived. According to the account of Evliya Čelebi in the seventeenth century, however, the minarets of Qusun were decorated with faience, and faience mosaics in blue, black, white and turquoise, like that at the top of al-Nasir's minarets, are .indeed one of the distinguishing elements of Ilkhanid Iranian architectural decoration.   The craftsman from Tabriz must therefore have been given the opportunity to apply his talents to the Sultan's building as well. Unlike Iranian minarets, al-Nasir's minarets are built in stone. In this context one should ask how far involved the Tabrizi craftsman was in the architecture of the two minarets, apart from designing their faience decoration. Meinecke has been able to demonstrate on the basis of an Iranian fourteenth-century miniature that the design of the minaret's bulbs originated in Tabriz. As in the case of Ibn Tulun's minaret built in stone from a foreign brick prototype, al-Nasir's example

Plate 26. The minaret of Sunqur al-Sa'di (Hasan Sadaqa)

demonstrates the Egyptian mason's ability to adopt new patterns while executing them in the technique and materials he was familiar with.

The mosque of al-Nasir Muhammad was built in 1318, then rebuilt, according to Maqrizi, in 1335. The sole surviving inscription, however, located on the western entrance, indicates the earlier date only. Traces of the original masonry of the mosque (fragments of the old crenellations, for example), show that during the second stage of construction the existing walls were heightened. Contrary to all Mamluk examples, the bases of the two minarets are below the present roof level of the mosque, indicating that they were built during the first stage of construction. Their staircases also terminate below the roof. The earlier date then is true for the lower part of the shaft, though the evidence does not exclude the possibility of modifications to the tops of the minarets during the restoration of 1335.

The bulbous structures surmounting the two minarets are similar, except that the bulb on the eastern minaret is set above an open hexagonal pavilion, while in the western minaret the bulbous structure alone forms the third story. Nearly all pre-Ottoman minarets in Cairo have open upper structures — either eight columns carrying the bulb, or the *mabkhara* — this western minaret of al-Nasir, the minaret of Bashtak (which might have been altered by restoration) and the so-called southern minaret being sole exceptions. In the case of al-Nasir Muhammad, the preference for a solid construction at the top must be explained by the desire to make the most of the *faience* decoration, a novelty at that time in Cairo.

While the location of the western minaret, near the main entrance of the mosque, is normal, the location of the other minaret, on the northern corner of the prayer hall, needs an explanation. The Citadel had been the residence of the sultans since the end of the Ayyubid period and contained not only this new mosque with the barracks of the Mamluks to its north, but also various residential structures including the official part of the royal complexes to the south. The western entrance of the mosque was the ceremonial one used by the Sultan coming from his apartments, while the northern one faced the dwellings of the Mamluks and served as a public entrance. The western minaret addressed the prayer call to the inhabitants of the royal apartments, from which it was quite visible, while the northern minaret was close to the ears of the more public quarters. The northern minaret carries an additional structure below the bulb, which makes it higher than the western one, a feature that allowed its blue faience decoration shining against the sky to be seen from the royal apartments as well, despite the distance and the angle of vision.

While the two minarets have similar faience-decorated tops, their shapes differ, the western minaret being carved, circular and tapering. The northern

80

Plate 27. The minarets of al-Nasir Muhammad at the Citadel

minaret is plain, rectangular at the first story and circular at the second; its parapets made of pierced stone slabs which run around the galleries of the *mu'adhdhin* are the earliest example of this type. They have a stylistic predecessor in the famous stone screens which decorate the mausoleum of Sanjar. The crenellation decorating the top is a rare feature on minarets; it can also be seen at Bashtak and Iljay al-Yusufi. The square shaft of the eastern minaret with its stalactite cornice recalls that of al-Baqli and the combination of square and circular sections in one shaft has already been seen at the minaret of Baybars al-Jashankir. Nevertheless, the two minarets of al-Nasir have a character unique in Cairene architecture.

The minaret of Amir Bashtak 737/1336

The massiveness of this minaret and its treatment of stone are almost Pharaonic. Only the minaret and a magnificent portal have survived of the original complex, which once included both a mosque and a *khanqa*. Maqrizi writes that Bashtak, one of the mightiest amirs of Sultan al-Nasir Muhammad, built a mosque at Qabuw al-Kirmani which overlooked the pond of Birkat al-Fil in the aristocratic residential quarter that covered the area occupied today by the quarter of

81

Hilmiyya, north of Sayyida Zaynab. The eastern side of the complex was bordered by a street running along the pond of Birkat al-Fil, while its western side, with the facade and the minaret, was bordered by the street of Qabuw al-Kirmani, running parallel to the Khalij, the Canal of Cairo. The mosque was on the eastern side of this street, but the *khanqa* was on the western, overlooking the Canal, and the two buildings were connected by an elevated passage over the street.

As in the case of Sanjar al-Jawli, the fact that the mosque was located between two equally prestigious streets, Qabuw al-Kirmani and that of Birkat al-Fil, finds its expression in the orientation of the inscriptions. The portal open to Qabuw al-Kirmani was on the axis of the building which disappeared a long time ago. The inscription bands on the minaret do not start on the portal side as usual, however, but rather on the eastern side, towards Birkat al-Fil. This side, Birkat al-Fil, was more urbanized than the street onto which the main portal opened, which is why Maqrizi describes the mosque as overlooking Birkat al-Fil, despite the location of the minaret and the portal, i.e., the main facade, on the building's opposite side. Further south along the same street is another building erected more than a century later, the mosque of Qaraqaja al-Hasani (1443), whose minaret also carries an inscription that starts on the back side, i.e., the side of Birkat al-Fil, instead of the portal side. It is not only these inscriptions, however, that indicate the urban context of Bashtak's mosque. As at the minaret of Sanjar, the minaret of Bashtak has an elaborate portal which addresses the viewer at the back of the mosque, leading to its staircase on the roof level. This portal is decorated with a stalactite cresting and states in its own inscription band that its construction was started in the month of Ramadan 736/1335 and completed in Rajab 737/1336. Sanjar's and Bashtak's are the only Mamluk minarets to include such a feature, and in both cases it is dictated by similar urban settings.

The deep carving in the middle section of the minaret of Bashtak is unique in Cairo. The small stone bulbs between the panels of the parapets at the *mu'adhdhin* galleries are carved, in the same manner as the bulbs on top of the minarets of Shaikhu and Sarghitmish, in an almond-shaped pattern. The third story is crowned by crenellations, some parts of which have preserved a carved decoration visible only from the roof of the mosque and with a powerful lens. Another unusual aspect of the minaret is that the third story is not open, but solid and plain. Hasan 'Abd al-Wahhab attributes this story to restoration done in the late Ottoman period, when the mosque was rebuilt. The masonry, however, looks the same all the way to the top of the minaret. The original stones may have been used to restore the top, as indicated by the crenellations which are partly carved and partly plain. Also the lack of stalactites at the top is very unusual for the Mamluk period and rather suggests that a later restoration took place, which seems to have respected the original proportions of the minaret.

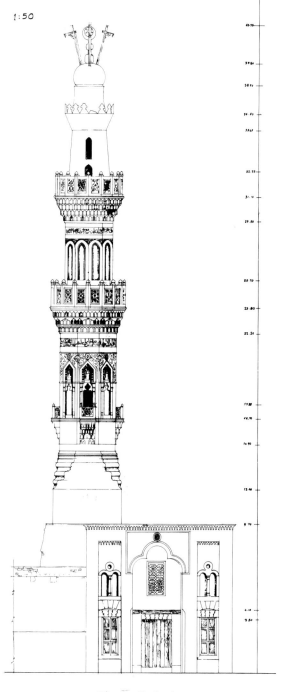

1:50

Fig. 9. Bashtak

Plate 28. Bashtak

The transitional zone of this minaret, i.e. the section between the square base and the octagonal shaft, is the earliest example of folded consoles carved as a transitional element, a device that will later influence the architecture of stone domes.

The minaret of Qusun 737/1337

The minaret of Qusun in the Suyuti cemetery on the southeastern side of the Citadel, an impressive rectangular stone shaft carrying an octagonal second story with a stone *mabkhara,* seems at first glance to be a free-standing structure. A closer look at the minaret, however, confirms that it was once attached to a building and, in fact, historical sources mention a monastery (*khanqa*) and a tomb built by Amir Qusun in this area. Crenellation at the rectangular section indicates the presence of the walls once attached to the minaret, and the entrance to the shaft, which is above this crenellation, shows the level of the roof, which must have been reached by a staircase outside the minaret shaft. Apart from this minaret, a mausoleum dome is all that survives of the funerary-religious complex of Qusun. It is located at some distance to the east of the minaret and is not

Plate 29. The minarets of Qusun (left) and al-Sultaniyya (right) with the Sultaniyya mausoleum domes between them

84

connected to it by any extant construction, though both the masonry and the inscriptions, on the two structures are complementary. The inscription bands on the dome and on the base of the minaret stand at the same level measured from the ground and contain verses from the same *Sura* (xxxvi), the verses on the minaret being from the beginning of the *Sura,* those on the dome from the middle. Taken with architectural arguments, the presence of verses from the same *Sura* on the two structures is evidence that both are parts of the same building, as has been demonstrated by Layla Ali Ibrahim in a study on this *khanqa.* Since inscriptions usually start on the right side of the facade, and minarets are usually attached to the facade, it has therefore been possible to reconstruct the plan of Qusun's *khanqa* basing the reconstruction on the parts of the inscription that are missing between the minaret and the dome. According to this reconstruction, it must have been a huge building, with two domes and proportions similar to those of the *khanqa* of Faraj Ibn Barquq. The minaret must have projected at the northwestern corner.

Beside the inscription from *Sura* xxxvi that runs from its base along all the exterior walls of the building, the minaret of Qusun carries four other inscription bands, one of them bearing the date 737, which is one year later than that given by Maqrizi for the construction of the complex. This discrepancy is not surprising, since the construction of a religious building usually began with the prayer hall, which was used immediately, often before the other structures were terminated, and the minaret was normally among the last parts to be built. Many foundation documents either do not include a description of the minaret or simply refer to its future construction, the foundation deeds being written during the course of the construction.

The stone *mabkhara* atop the minaret of Qusun has been considered by Kessler as the prototype for later stone dome architecture, most of the *mabkharas* surviving in Cairo having been built in brick. Together with that of Ibn Tulun added by Lajin, the *mabkharas* of Qusun and Tankizbugha are exceptions.

The Southern minaret 740s/1340s

The "Southern" minaret is an extraordinary construction displaying ambitious proportions and a magnificent treatment of stone. Located in the Bahri Mamluk (or Suyuti cemetery), it has been called the Southern minaret because it stands to the south of a group of monuments including the convent of Qusun and the Sultaniyya tomb and is the only surviving structure of the unidentified building to which it was attached. (Its staircase starts at a level that must have been that of the roof of the building.)

Fig. 10. Qusun   Fig. 11. "Southern" minaret

The style of the minaret and its size attribute it to the first half of the fourteenth century. During this period, the reign of Sultan al-Nasir Muhammad, a great number of religious-funeral buildings were erected in this area and therefore, unless a document precisely identifying the Southern minaret comes to light, it is useless to speculate about its sponsor. As for its style, this minaret is not identical to any other Cairene minaret, though its proportions recall Bashtak, Aqsunqur and Qusun. Some details of its decoration, like the treatment of the stalactites below the small balconies of the octagonal section, the hoods of the arched panels, which alternate carved and plain, and the stalactites of the upper gallery, recall the smaller minaret of Aydumur al-Bahlawan (1347) at Jamaliyya. Atypical is the solid third story, which suggests that it probably once carried a fourth story in the form of the usual open structure; the bulb added recently without the intermediary of such a structure does not seem to fit, and we have seen that the minaret of Aqsunqur originally had four, not three stories.

An original feature can be seen in the treatment of the octagonal third story, where vestiges of capitals and column bases stand at each of the eight corners, indicating missing colonettes, some of which are visible in a drawing made by Bourgoin. A similar arrangement can be seen at the *mabkhara* added by Lajin to the minaret of Ibn Tulun. Another unusual combination is the octagonal third story on top of a circular second story: usually the reverse arrangement is the case.

The minaret of Altinbugha al-Maridani 740/1340

The minaret at the mosque of al-Maridani is the earliest existing minaret with an entirely octagonal shaft, which Creswell claims must be due to some foreign influence. And indeed, octagonal minarets existed earlier in Mesopotamia and were later erected in Syria. Among these was one built by Altinbugha al-Maridani, who according to Creswell must have introduced this pattern into Egypt.

We have seen, however, that the helmet on minarets was usually carried by an octagonal structure, which became increasingly elongated from one minaret to the next until the entire second story took the shape of an octagonal shaft. We have also seen how the octagonal shaft with keel-arched niches supporting the helmet on top of the minaret was in a later phase transferred to form the first story of the minaret, as at Bashtak and Aqbugha. If at the beginning of the fourteenth century we already have octagonal first stories and octagonal upper stories, is it any wonder that the highly imaginative Cairene architect should finally build minarets with all three stories octagonal? Why should a foreign prototype have been required?

The minaret of al-Maridani was built by the royal chief-architect, Mu'allim al-Suyufi — the same man who built the minaret of Aqbugha at al-Azhar — but the minarets of Aqbugha and al-Maridani are not identical. The only thing they have in common, in fact, is the *ablaq* (two-colored) inlaid stone work that decorates both shafts.

The upper structure of the minaret of al-Maridani has been restored, but fortunately the new work followed traces of the original bulb, which were still extant when restoration was undertaken. Since the top of Aqbugha's minaret disappeared long before it was restored (by the Comite de conservation des monuments d'art arabe, which functioned from 1882 to 1954), the minaret of al-Maridani thus has the earliest existing top composed of a stone bulb supported by columns.

The minaret stands at the corner of the mosque on the left side of the entrance vault. A close look at the stones of the wall added to reinforce the buttress of the minaret shows that the masonry is different from that of the rest of the mosque. This wall also hides part of an inscription band, which starts on the right side of the portal and continues to the left around the building and must therefore be a later addition.

Similar to the minaret of al-Maridani are the minarets of Shaikhu (1345-1351) Sarghitmish (1356), Tatar al-Hijaziyya (1360), Sultan Hasan (1363) and Sultaniyya (late fourteenth century), all of which are octagonal with shafts decorated in inlaid stone patterns of two colors (*ablaq*) and sometimes with a shallow relief carving. The minarets of Umm al-Sultan Sha'ban (1369) and Sultan Barquq (1386) differ in that they are adorned in the middle section with carving, which in the fifteenth century will replace inlaid stone decoration.

The minaret of Aqsunqur 748/1347

The minaret of Aqsunqur at the so-called Blue Mosque is one of the most impressive Cairene minarets in shape, proportions and placement. It is also a rare example of a minaret totally circular in section from the base to the top.

This minaret does not stand at the portal, but at a more strategic location, the southern corner, projecting into the street and thus dominating the southern part of Bab al-Wazir Avenue, which starts at the Citadel and leads to Bab Zuwayla. It is small wonder that this minaret has often been depicted by artists of the nineteenth century, to whom we owe information of special interest.

Like many other minarets, this one has a restored third story, and today it shows us an undistinguished arrangement with restoration at the top. Originally, however, it must have been quite different: three drawings made by prominent illustrators of nineteenth century Cairo, Roberts, Coste and Girault de Prangey, depict the minaret of Aqsunqur with four stories instead of three — the only documented case in Cairo, apart from the rectangular minaret of Sultan al-Ghuri, though such four-story minarets were built in the provinces. Atop the octagonal open structure we see today as the third story, there once stood another open structure, made of columns carrying stalactites, which supported a bulb.

Plate 30 (*left*). The "Southern" minaret (with a restored top)

Plate 31 (*right*). The minaret of Altinbugha al-Maridani

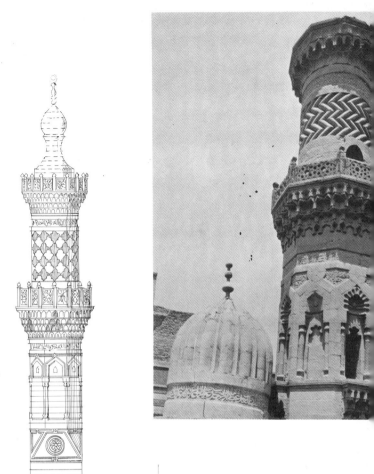

Fig. 12 (*left*). Aqbugha (1340)

Plate 32 (*right*). The minaret of Aydu
al-Bahlawan (1346)

Fig. 13 (*left*). Aqsunqur (*de Prangey*)

Plate 33 (*right*).   The minaret of
Aqsunqur

Fig. 14 (*left*). Aqsunqur (*Coste*)

Plate 34 (*right*). The minaret of Aqsunqur (
depicted last century by Roberts, with
stories

Plate 35. The minaret of Arghunshah
al-Isma'ili (1347)

Plate 36. The minaret of Manjaq al-
Yusufi (al-Silahdar) with a restored
mabkhara

The minaret of Manjaq al-Yusufi (al-Silahdar) 750-51/1349-50

This minaret, located on the northern side of the Citadel, is almost all that is left of the mosque of Manjaq. Since its staircase starts at ground level, it was probably free-standing at the time of its construction. The whole upper part of the minaret is modern, but it is likely that the Comité restored it from an illustration by Roberts which depicted it before its top collapsed. It is the only example of a combination of an octagonal shaft with a *mabkhara* cap. The treatment of the galleries with vertical and horizontal moldings instead of stalactites is the same as on the minarets of Shaikhu.

The minarets of Shaikhu 750-756/1349-55

Amir Shaikhu first built, on the northern side of Saliba Street, a mosque with a mausoleum for himself. The mosque has a minaret over the portal and is dated 750 (1349). Six years later he erected a large *khanqa* across the street, and a minaret was added to the *khanqa* to create a symmetrical composition: two identical portals, each surmounted by a minaret, facing each other across the

93

1:50

Fig. 15. Manjaq al-Yusufi

Plate 37. The minarets of Shaikhu, mosque to the right, *khanqa* to the left

street. A model may have been provided by Bashtak whose *khanqa* and mosque were on opposites sides of a street, though there is not enough left of Bashtak's complex to establish any further similarity. The interesting feature of Shaikhu's complex is that the symmetry of these portals with their minarets framing the street like a gate has the effect of transforming the street itself—an important processional road leading from the Citadel to the southern and western outskirts of the city—into a part of the religious complex.

Both minarets of Shaikhu are entirely octagonal constructions decorated with shallow relief carving and inlaid stones. The bulbs crowning each minaret rest on necks carved with Quranic inscriptions, a feature they share only with the minarets of al-Nasir at the Citadel. Both examples being among the rare bulbs to have survived in their original outlook, we can not exclude the possibility that there was a tradition to decorate the bulbs on top of minarets. The bulbs at Shaikhu's minarets are carved in an almond-shape pattern that can also be seen at the minaret of Sarghitmish, nearby on the same street. Unusual is the absence of stalactites beneath the *mu'adhdhin* galleries, where moldings have been used instead, a horizontal one at the lower gallery, and a vertical one at the upper. A vertical molding of this type can be seen at the top of the minaret of Qalawun added by his son al-Nasir.

The two minarets of Shaikhu are not quite identical, differing not only in the pattern of their carving, but also in their transitional zones. The transitional zone of the minaret attached to the mosque has a pyramidal shape, while that of the minaret at the *khanqa* consists of triangles pointing downwards. Carved on the eastern face of the lower inscription band of the mosque minaret is a date that is unfortunately almost illegible. The inscription of the *khanqa* minaret is a *Sura*, rarely used on minarets, which refers to the pilgrimage to Mecca. Shaikhu himself is not reported to have fulfilled the pilgrimage commandment, but the shaikh of his *khanqa* most probably did.

The minarets of Sultan Hasan 757/1356

The mosque of Sultan Hasan was planned to have four minarets, two at the portal in addition to the two in the location we see today. The treatment of the portal closely resembles that in Anatolian *madrasas*, which suggests that the minarets were probably planned to flank the portal in the Anatolian style. Only one of the minarets at the portal was ever erected. When it collapsed shortly after its completion, killing two hundred children — orphans studying in a nearby school — the accident was considered as a bad omen, and the second minaret was never built. Poems were written to commemorate the tragedy, which was interpreted as an act of God, rather than the result of a structural deficiency, and in fact, it was only thirty days after the fall of the minaret that Sultan Hasan himself was killed.

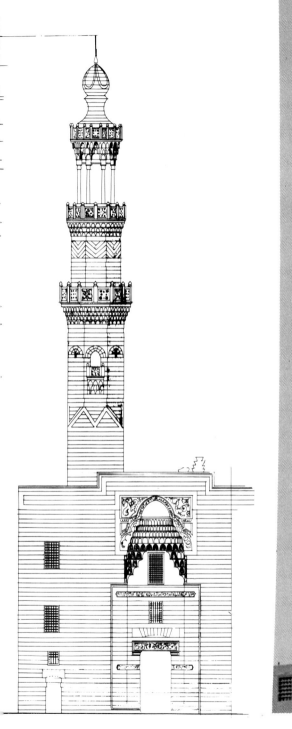

Fig. 16. Sarghitmish (1356)

Plate 38. The minaret of
Sarghitmish (1356)

Much later, in 1070 (1659), one of the minarets on the southeastern wall collapsed during Friday prayers, when the mosque was filled to capacity. The minaret fell outwards from the mosque, however, and only two people, a man and a woman, were killed by the falling stones, which were strewn for some distance around the mosque. The seventeenth century Moroccan traveller al-'Ayyashi (cited by al-Warthilani), saw this collapsed minaret during his passage through Egypt on his way to Mecca. On his return from the pilgrimage he was astonished to find that the ruined minaret had been replaced by the structure which stands today at the northeastern corner of the mosque. Full of admiration for the zeal of the Egyptians and the care they took to restore their buildings, al-'Ayyashi wrote that a sum of sixty *kis* was spent alone on the task of collecting the fallen stones for re-use in the reconstruction of the minaret, adding "imagine then the expense of the reconstruction itself!" He also deplored the condition of the monuments in his own country, which no one bothered to maintain. He seems not to have noticed how inferior the new version looked compared to the original!

The mosque of Sultan Hasan has two important facades — the northern facade on Suq al-Silah with its gigantic portal, and the eastern facade, which is that of the mausoleum dome, flanked by the two minarets and facing the Citadel. The position of the mosque, just below the Citadel (the residence of the Sultans) and its location on the Rumayla Square, overlooking the great hippodrome, center of festivals and tournaments, are most important for an understanding of its layout. The position of the mosque in relation to the Citadel explains the angle at which the portal turns: its magnificence could not escape the eyes of the Sultan as he looked down from his castle which stood high above, close to the place where today the mosque of Muhammad 'Ali stands. Proximity to the Citadel, also explains why the dome of the mausoleum, originally a bulbous structure higher than the restored dome we see today, was set beyond the prayer hall in the direction of prayer, a feature unusual in Mamluk architecture. It thus dominated the skyline seen by royal eyes looking down from the hill. It was undoubtedly to preserve this domination that the minarets were built to either side of the mausoleum, an arrangement unique in Mamluk architecture.

Proximity to the Citadel, moreover, explains the vicissitudes the building has gone through: its massive walls placed in such a location led to its being used quite often as a fortress, a base for attack and a center of resistance against the official power ensconced in the Citadel. When rebelling Mamluks at the end of the fourteenth century installed themselves in the minarets, for example, from which they could shoot at the Citadel, Sultan Barquq was prompted to destroy the staircases and to block the main entrance, so that the building had to be entered through the windows and the *mu'adhdhin*s were obliged to perform the call to prayer in front of the mosque. In 1422, the minarets were again used for the *adhan,* upon the installation of new staircases to the roof, which were once more

Plate 39. The minarets of Sultan Hasan (14th and 17th centuries)

destroyed during a rebellion in 1438. Even the crescent on top of the southern minaret suffered under such violence and had to be restored in 1453, as Ibn Taghribirdi relates. During the Ottoman period, pitched battles between different corps of the army were fought in the space defined by the minarets of Sultan Hasan and those of the surrounding mosques and the Citadel, to the extent that the mosque was closed for fifty-one years, and the mausoleum dome, punctured and weakened by the hail of cannonballs, collapsed.

Yet the mosque of Sultan Hasan was also the scene of less violent displays. In 1425, a Persian merchant stretched a rope between the two minarets upon which he walked, sat and performed various kinds of acrobatics. Maqrizi devotes an entire page of his chronicle to a description of the Persian's wondrous pirouettes. Another acrobat stretched a rope between one of the minarets of Sultan Hasan and a place within the Citadel, over which he traveled to and fro entertaining people from all parts of Cairo including the Sultan, who generously rewarded him for his performance. Yet another is recorded to have performed similar feats, jumping from the rope to the apex of the lead-covered dome "as if he were of air" on a day so foul that trees were almost uprooted by wind and not even birds could fly!

Fig. 17. Sultan Hasan

As for the architectural aspect of the Sultan Hasan minarets, the southern one is the highest minaret of medieval Cairo (about eighty meters); it has an entirely octagonal shape, and the shaft is decorated with inlaid stone work. The northern minaret, which was rebuilt in the seventeenth century, is one of the few attempts made in the Ottoman period to build minarets in the Mamluk style.

Such attempts were made in the event that a Mamluk minaret had to be replaced (normally it was preferred to attach minarets of Ottoman style to new mosques). Unfortunately, the quality of the reconstruction remained far below that of the original; symmetry was no longer achieved: the rebuilt minaret is smaller, its stalactites of poor quality, and its bulb is set above the second story without the support of the usual graceful eight-column, stalactite-crowned Mamluk pavillion. A glance at the unequal pair makes clear that the Ottoman craftsmen had abandoned the carving of elaborate stalactites, together with the art of the lofty three-storied minaret, once mastered by Mamluk architects.

The minaret at the mausoleum of Sultaniyya 1360s

The twin bulbous domes of the mausoleum popularly called al-Sultaniyya look as exotic as they are mysterious. No name or date have survived to tell about their founder or their origin. Creswell has attributed them to the early fifteenth century because of their similarity with the Timurid mausoleum domes at Samarqand built at that time, which according to him must have inspired the architecture of the Sultaniyya. However, the minaret attached to the complex is similar to that of Sultan Hasan and others built in the second half of the fourteenth century. Also the domes, bulbous with a high drum adorned with a stalactite cornice at its top, and each including an interior dome, are not unrelated to the dome of Sarghitmish (1356). In an interesting thesis, Farida Maqar has attributed this complex to the mother of Sultan Hasan and assigned it to the third quarter of the fourteenth century. As far as the style of the minaret is concerned, this date is quite adequate.

The minaret of Tankizbugha 764/1362

This *khanqa* with a domed mausoleum is located on a hill on the southeastern side of the Qaytbay cemetery. The building and its location have an austerity which suits its function as a monastery. Its stone minaret is one of the *mabkhara* type — the latest surviving example — but its shape is reduced and consists of only two stories. An almost undecorated rectangular shaft carries an octagonal section pierced on all faces and adorned with a broad band of Quranic inscription. The ribbed helmet rests on a cornice that displays a peculiar kind of stalactite resembling thorns, similar to stalactites on a stone dome built by the same amir south of the Citadel and on a few other minarets, e.g. those of Sultan Hasan, Qusun, Inal and Azdumur. The general composition of the minaret of Tankizbugha resembles that of the minarets of al-Baqli and Fatima Khatun, both of which were built much earlier (1284 and 1297). It thus demonstrates that in spite of the evolution of Cairene minarets from two-story to three-story composition, the earlier type was not totally abandoned. Such archaism is not unusual in Mamluk architecture.

101

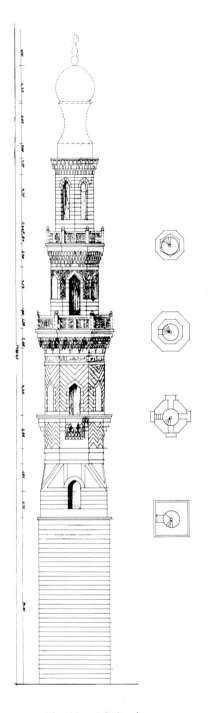

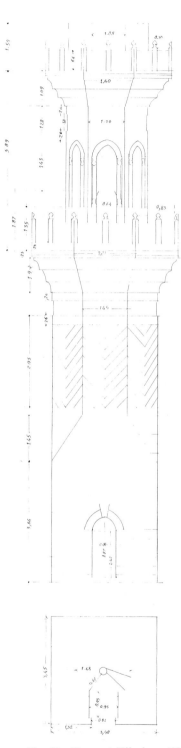

Fig. 18. al-Sultaniyya
Fig. 19. Tatar al-Hijaziyya (1360)

Plate 40. The minaret of Tatar al-Hijaziyya (1360) (*Photo: Antiquity Department*)

Plate 41. The minaret of Tankizbugha

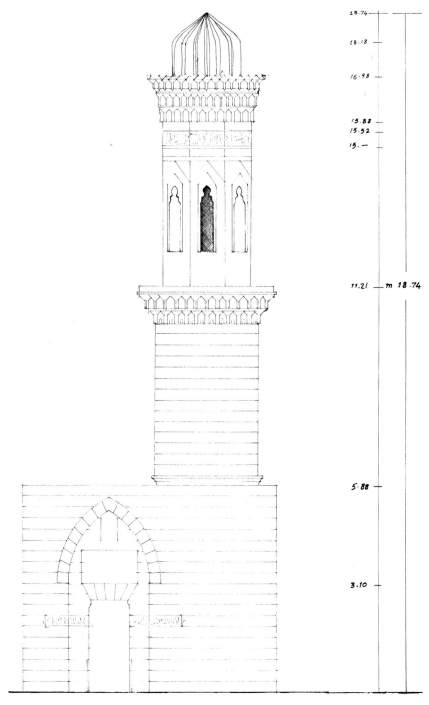

18.74

18.18

16.98

15.88
15.52
15.—

11.21 — m 18.74

5.88

3.10

Fig. 20. Tankizbugha

Plate 42. The minaret of Umm al-Sultan Sha‘ban (1368-9)

The minaret of Asanbugha 772/1370

We have seen that an octagonal section was first adopted in Cairene minarets when the architect tried to combine a square with a circular section — the octagonal shaft being created as a transition between the square base and the circular middle shaft—initially at Bashtak and Aqbugha. And indeed, the combination of the square and circular forms, without the use of an octagonal intermediate shaft, would result in something like the northern minaret of al-Nasir Muhammad at the Citadel or the minaret of Baybars al-Jashankir. It would appear, however, that an unmediated change of shape did not find great favor, for it was not widely used.

A minaret could also combine the triangular and the hexagonal, and in fact two examples from the fourteenth and fifteenth centuries have survived. The fourteenth century example is the minaret at the mosque of Asanbugha built in

105

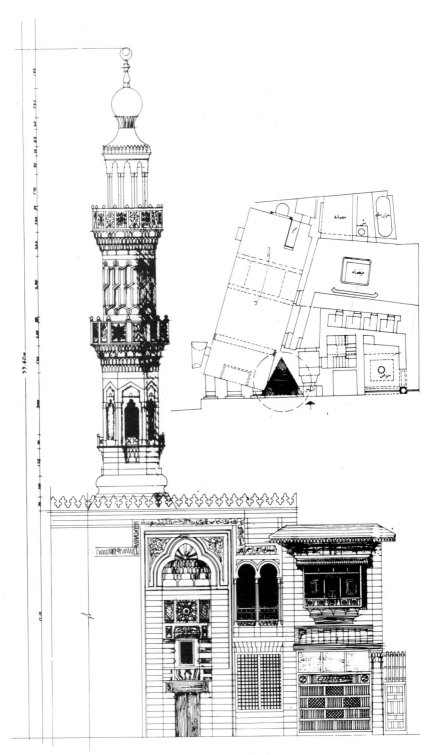

Fig. 21. Asanbugha

Plate 43. The minaret of Asanbugha

Plate 44.   The minaret of Iljay al-Yusufi (1373)

Plate 45. The minaret of the *madrasa* of Barquq

1370, one of the most exquisite minarets in Cairo. The anomaly of its shape must be attributed to structural rather than stylistic or esthetic considerations, but it is not easy to visualize the determinants unless one stands on the roof of the mosque. In all likelihood, having given his building the proper Mecca orientation, having located the *sabil-kuttab* at the corner (as was the custom), and having arranged the entrance so that it did not open directly into the mosque, the architect found that the only space overlooking the street for the base of the minaret was a triangle too small for a square to be cut from it. In order to exploit this space to the utmost, the architect, therefore, gave the minaret a triangular base, and found a hexagonal section the best choice for a transition into the circular upper story. The minaret of Asanbugha is a masterpiece of proportions and decoration as well as of architectural innovation. The bulb at the top of the minaret and the delicate petal motif supporting it display fine craftmanship; and the carved decoration of the middle shaft, with a complex interlacing design that appears from surviving monuments to be the first of its kind deserves special mention. It seems to have been judged quite pleasing, for it was later used on minarets more than any other such motif — at Barquq's mausoleum, at Barsbay's *madrasa,* the minaret of Qaraqaja al-Hasani and the minaret of Qanim al-Tajir (no longer extant) — and was also adopted on domes, e.g. the domes of Umm al-Ashraf (1430's) and Taghribirdi (1440).

The minaret at the "madrasa" of Sultan Barquq 788/1386

The location of this minaret adjoining the mausoleum dome at the northern edge of the facade has its parallel in the minaret of Sultan Qalawun, which is separated from that of Barquq only by the *madrasa* of al-Nasir. The minaret of Barquq is octagonal like most of the minarets of the period. Its decoration combines the inlaid stone work fashionable in the fourteenth century with the carving preferred in the fifteenth. Although it is no longer visible under layers of dust, there is marble inlaid in the middle section. The intersecting carved circles represent a variation on the theme of intersecting arches displayed on the minarets of Qalawun and Asanbugha.

The minaret of Mahmud al-Kurdi 797/1395

This is one of the few examples of an entirely circular minaret, the first story of which is plain, the second ribbed. The construction is of brick. Other minarets of circular shape are the northern minaret of al-Hakim, the western minaret of al-Nasir Muhammad at the Citadel and the minaret of Aqsunqur.

Plate 46. The minaret of Mahmud al-
Kurdi

Plate 47. The minaret attached to the
mosque of al-Aqmar (added by Amir
Yalbugha al-Salimi)

Plate 48. The minaret of al-Ruway
(1400s)

The minaret at the mosque of al-Aqmar 800/1397

No original minaret has survived at the mosque of al-Aqmar built in the Fatimid
period (1125). It was heavily restored at the end of the fourteenth century, and a
minaret was added to it by Amir Yalbugha al-Salimi in 1397, as an inscription slab
states. This minaret is reported to have been pulled down in 1412 when it started
leaning, but the present structure seems to include its first story which is a brick
construction still partly covered with carved stucco bearing a chevron pattern like
the one on the western minaret of al-Nasir Muhammad at the Citadel. A finely
carved molding includes raised and pierced bosses of stucco, similar to *repoussé*
metal work, a type of stucco work that exists otherwise in Cairo only at the prayer
niche of the *madrasa* of al-Nasir Muhammad in the Coppersmiths street.

112

Plate 49. The minarets at the *khanqa* of Faraj Ibn Barquq

The minarets at the khanqa of Faraj Ibn Barquq 813/1411

The funeral complex of Faraj Ibn Barquq, built for his father in the northern cemetery, is one of the most remarkable constructions of medieval Cairo. The complex includes two identical domes as well as two identical minarets. The western facade thus displays the two minarets, the northern and the southern each present a minaret and a dome, and the eastern is dominated by the two funeral domes flanking a smaller dome above the prayer niche of the mosque.

The minarets at the *khanqa* of Faraj have a rectangular first story which carries a circular second one without transition. This combination follows the model of al-Nasir's northern minaret and that of Qanibay al-Sharkasi, and will be repeated at the minarets of Barsbay, which are copies of Faraj's minarets.

113

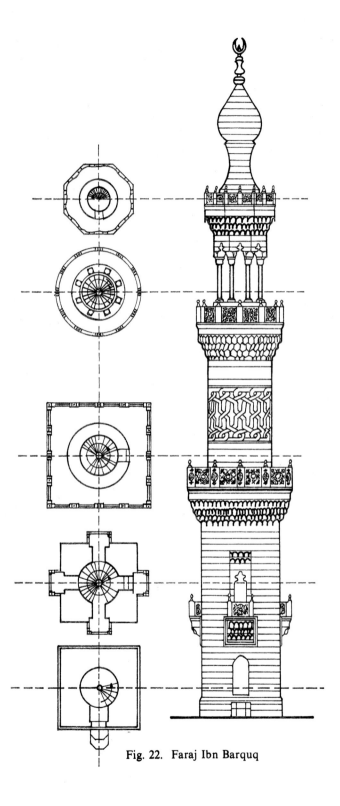

Fig. 22. Faraj Ibn Barquq

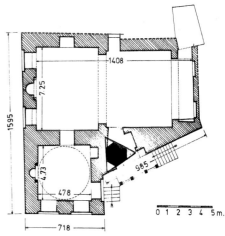

Plate 50 (*left*). The minaret of Qanibay al-Muhammadi

Fig. 23 (*right*). Qanibay al-Muhammadi

The minaret of Qanibay al-Muhammadi 816/1413

The only remarkable feature of this structure is the triangular base combined with a hexagonal first story. The architect of this minaret was not as capable, however, as the architect who designed the minaret of Asanbugha, the earlier minaret with a triangular base. Qanibay's combination of a triangular base with a hexagonal shaft and an octagonal second story is less harmonious than the ensemble at Asanbugha, where the second story is circular. The carving, as on the nearby dome, has a zig-zag motif like the minaret of al-Mu'ayyad.

The architect's reason for using a triangular base was, as in the case of Asanbugha, lack of space. Accurate Mecca-orientation of the prayer hall and the dome of the adjacent mausoleum overlooking the street left limited space in the L-shaped lot for both a bent entrance and a minaret. Ultimately only a triangle between the portal and the dome was left for the minaret.

115

The minarets of al-Mu'ayyad Shaikh 822-23/1419-20

Standing like a pair of guardians on each of the towers of Bab Zuwayla, the minarets of al-Mu'ayyad seem to confirm Cairo's byname "*al-Mahrusa*", the well-protected. Attached to the southern gate, they faced the processions coming down from the Citadel into the heart of the capital, which by that time had expanded beyond Bab Zuwayla into the southern quarters; they thus were the most prominently located minarets of the old city. At this gate a loggia is built, which must have been used by the royal orchestra to announce processions or the arrival of a prominent person. The historians inform us, however, that the location of al-Mu'ayyad's mosque was chosen not — as one might think from looking at the minarets — according to esthetic or urban considerations, but as a result of al-Mu'ayyad's having been imprisoned in one of the worst jails of medieval Cairo. He made a vow that if he came out of it alive he would build a mosque on the site. He did, and the towers of Bab Zuwayla, built at the end of the eleventh century, offered themselves as appropriate buttresses for the mosque's minarets.

Grafting the two new minarets onto the existing towers, however, did not make things any easier for the architect. Because it began to lean shortly after it was erected, one of the minarets had to be dismantled, an event that the poets of the day saw as full of meaning: the architectural failure was proof of an evil eye on the minaret or a curse on the old gate.

When he finally succeeded in erecting two identical minarets, the architect, Muhammad Ibn al-Qazzaz, found his achievement worth a signature. The twin minarets are both signed and dated 822 and 823H., the only examples so far known of an architect's signature in medieval Cairo, though there is another such signature in Egypt on a minaret near Aswan dating from the Abbasid or Fatimid period which has been deciphered by Hasan al-Hawwari. Muhammad Ibn al-Qazzaz's inscription specifies that he built the minarets, but it is not clear what if any contribution he made to the rest of the mosque.

The twin minarets of Bab Zuwayla are remarkable for their slenderness, but their decoration is similar to that on the minarets of Umm al-Sultan Sha'ban (1369), Qanibay al-Muhammadi (1413), Qadi 'Abd al-Basit (1420) and Tamim al-Rasafi (fifteenth century). Until the nineteenth century a third minaret—mentioned in the foundation deed of the mosque—stood near the northern portal. It was apparently different from the other two, since the historian al-Jawhari describes it as unique.

Plate 51. The minarets of al-Mu'ayyad at Bab Zuwayla

Fig. 24. al-Mu'ayyad at Bab Zuwayla

The minaret of Qadi 'Abd al-Basit 823/1420

This minaret looks exactly like those of al-Mu'ayyad built at the same time. Its inscription deserves mention since it is from the *Sura* of the Pilgrimage (XX, 17-18). Qadi 'Abd al-Basit accomplished the pilgrimage to Mecca and was the Nazir al-Kiswa, the amir in charge of the yearly dispatch of the *Ka'ba* covering from Egypt with the pilgrimage caravan, a tradition the Mamluk sultans considered their exclusive privilege. (See Van Berchem: Matériaux pour un Corpus Inscriptionum Arabicarum, III, p.344.)

Plate 52. The minaret of Qadi 'Abd al-Basit

Plate 53. The minaret of the *madrasa* of al-Ashraf Barsbay at the Coppersmiths' (1425)

Plate 54.   The minaret of Janibay
(1426-7)

Plate 55.   The minaret of Fayruz
(1426-7)

Plate 56 (*left*). The minaret of Taghribī
(1440)

Plate 57 (*right*). The minaret of Qanibay
Sharkasi (1442)

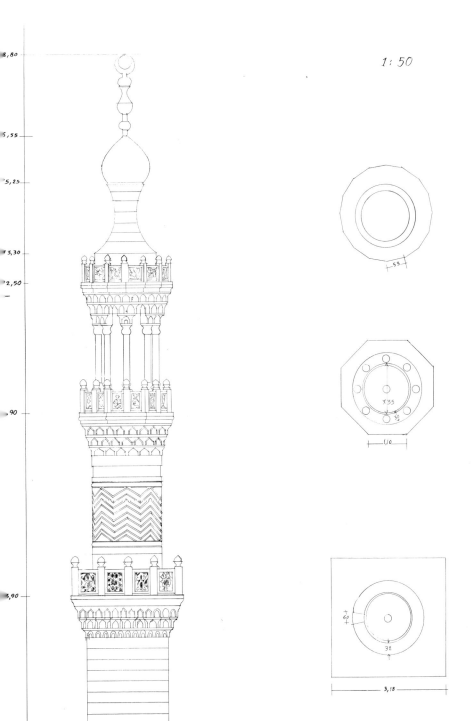

Fig. 25. Qanibay al-Sharkasi (1442)

Plate 58 (*left*). The minaret of Qaraqaja al-Hasani (1442), with bridge connecting it to the roof of the mosque

Plate 59 (*right*). The minaret of Qadi Yahya Zayn al-Din on al-Azhar Street (only the first story is original)

The minarets of Qadi Yahya Zayn al-Din 848-56/1444-1452-3

Three mosques in Cairo are attributed to Qadi Yahya Zayn al-Din and were built during the reign of Sultan Jaqmaq. The site of the earliest, dated 848 (1444) is in al-Azhar Street near what was once the Khalij or canal of Cairo. It has been heavily restored; the minaret with its blue inlaid arrows has been rebuilt, and only the first octagonal story, with the inscription band, is original.

The minaret at the mosque of Qadi Yahya at Bulaq (852-3/1448-9), of which no more than the first story has been preserved, affords some archeological interest because of the unusual device used to decorate the base of the gallery: instead of the customary stalactites, the carving displays a lozenge motif, which was to be imitated later at the minaret attached to the *madrasa* of Sultan Qaytbay at Qal'at al-Kabsh.

Finally, the minaret at the mosque of Qadi Yahya at Habbaniyya (856/1452-3), like that of Jaqmaq, has only a first story in stone, the upper part being of plastered wood. The columns at the top were removed decades ago by the Comité for reasons of safety.

125

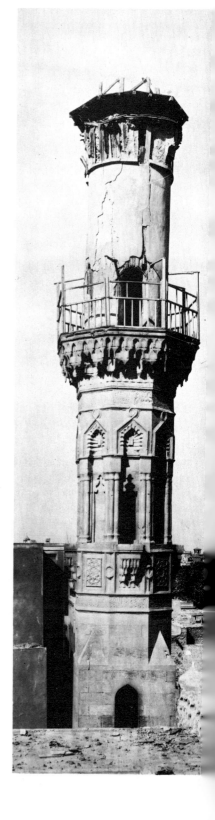

Plate 60 (*left*). The minaret of Qadi Yahya
Zayn al-Din at Bulaq

Plate 61 (*right*). The minaret of Qadi Yahya
Zayn al-Din at Habbaniyya

Plate 62. The minaret of Lajin al-Sayfi; the second story is Ottoman

The minarets of the reign of Sultan Jaqmaq 842-57/1438-53

Three mosques in Cairo are attributed to Sultan al-Zahir Jaqmaq. Of the earliest dated 1449, located at the Marasina Street (Lajin al-Sayfi, Index 217), only an octagonal first story has survived of the original minaret with a stalactite cornice. It has no inscription and offers no particular archeological interest. The second building is a *madrasa* (Index 180) dated 1451. Creswell describes its interior as "mean and shabby", which is also true of its minaret. Located at the northeastern corner of the building, it does not follow the facade alignment, but follows instead the Mecca orientation. It lacks any esthetic interest and is the only royal minaret of this period not to be built entirely in stone, its second story being made of plastered wood. The third building of Jaqmaq at Dayr al-Nahas (Index 317) near Fustat has disappeared, but a photograph by Creswell of its minaret exists (see plate 112). It was a brick construction of no special interest.

Sultan Jaqmaq was not a friend of the arts: in his extreme orthodoxy he prohibited shadow plays as well as all kinds of other entertainments. It is obvious — and not surprising — that he did not care for architectural beauty either.

The minaret at the religious-funerary complex of Sultan Inal 855-58/1451-54

A glance at the facade of this complex in the northern cemetery suffices to reveal an irregularity in its composition which is confirmed by epigraphy stating different dates for each part. When still an amir, Inal built himself a modest mausoleum, dated 1451 according to an inscription band on its facade. At stages in his rising career, the complex was expanded. In 1453, after he became sultan, a large convent was erected. A *madrasa* was later added, completed in 1456.

The minaret almost certainly existed before the *madrasa* was erected. Its octagonal first story begins far below the *madrasa*'s roof level, indicating that the *madrasa* was built later. The bases of the minaret and the mausoleum dome, however, seem to correspond to the same stage of construction, as they both end at the same level. The columns at three of the four corners of the minaret on street level suggest that it was once free-standing on three sides, while the fourth side was connected to a wall.

Funerary buildings without a religious function, such as that of a Friday mosque, college or monastery, could also have minarets attached to them. Therefore it would not be surprising that the minaret of Inal was built together

128

Plate 63. The minaret of the *madrasa* of Jaqmaq

Plate 64. The minaret at the complex of Sultan Inal

with the mausoleum dome before the *khanqa* and *madrasa* were added. Of course the mausoleum would have a prayer hall attached to it. Both the modest proportions of Inal's minaret and the low height of its buttress suggest that it predates the *madrasa* and is in all likelihood contemporary with the mausoleum.

The minaret of Amir Husayn 867/1462

The original minaret of Amir Husayn (1319) is recorded in the chronicle of Ibn Iyas as having collapsed, struck by a storm. It must have been rebuilt within the same period, as the style of the present structure indicates. The carving of the middle section resembles that of the minaret of al-Khatiri (1337), al-'Alaya (fifteenth century) and Inal (1456). The original location was also respected: Maqrizi writes that the minaret—like the present structure—stood above the portal.

130

Plate 65 (*facing page, left*). The minaret added to the mosque of Amir Husayn in 1462

Fig. 26 (*right*). Amir Husayn, rebuilt after 1462

The minaret of Sidi Madyan 872/1465

This minaret stands at the corner of the mosque, not exactly following its alignment, but placed at an angle across the corner. The minaret of Sidi Madyan happens to be mentioned in the biography of this Sufi Shaikh. Sha'rani reports that after the minaret was erected it started to lean, scaring the people of the quarter, so that the architects agreed upon the necessity of pulling it down. Shaikh Madyan, however, found a better solution: he went to the minaret, and, leaning his back on its shaft, started shaking it until it regained its upright position which it has maintained until today.

The minaret in the reign of Sultan al-Ashraf Qaytbay 1468-95

During the long reign of al-Ashraf Qaytbay, the second half of the fifteenth century witnesses a period of intense building activity. Like al-Nasir Muhammad, Qaytbay ruled long enough to achieve great architectural ambitions. It was during his time that Mamluk stone carving reached its apogee.

Buildings from that period are on a modest scale—the city of Cairo having become densely crowded with religious and commercial structures—but are graceful, even exquisite in their proportions, especially their minarets. Unlike the reign of al-Nasir Muhammad, no innovations of importance occur under Qaytbay; no traces of foreign craftsmen can be detected and forms are settled without the disturbance of exotic elements.

The minaret of this period is a stone construction with an octagonal first story, a circular middle section, and a third story composed of the slender stone columns that carry the bulb. No *mabkhara* tops exist from this period. Carving is lavishly used to decorate the niches, the colonettes and the panels of the octagonal section. Moldings run around the richly carved sides of the base.

In the fourteenth century, each minaret had been decorated with a different pattern of inlaid stone in the middle section; now it is the carving that varies from one minaret to the other. Both floral and geometrical designs are used and sometimes a combination of both. Inscription bands are abundant, usually Koranic texts, but sometimes including names and titles of the founder, as in the cases of Qaytbay at al-Azhar, Mughulbay Taz, Yashbak min Mahdi at the mosque of Imam al-Layth, and Azbak al-Yusufi.

The minaret of Qaytbay at his *madrasa* in the quarter of Qal'at al-Kabsh (1475) presents a slight anomaly: the first story is reduced, and the first gallery does not rest on stalactites as would be usual, but is supportd by an octagonal base that starts from the foot of the minaret and widens to carry it. This octagonal base

Plate 66. The minaret of Sidi Madyan

is decorated with carving that recalls the minaret of Qadi Yahya at Bulaq, where a similar structure is also used in place of stalactites below the first gallery.

The minaret that Yashbak min Mahdi added at the mosque of Imam al-Layth, dated 1479, and the minaret of Qaytbay on the island of Rawda also have no stalactites below the first gallery, while the minaret of Qaytbay at Rawda (1490) is plain in the middle section and has no columns on the top. Creswell attributes the molding beneath the second gallery to nineteenth-century restoration after the mosque was severely damaged by a fire in 1851.

The minaret of Yashbak min Mahdi at the shrine of Imam al-Layth is a free-standing construction located on the southwestern side of the mosque and is built over a public passage that used to lead to the mosque from the street, like the minaret of al-Salih Najm al-Din.

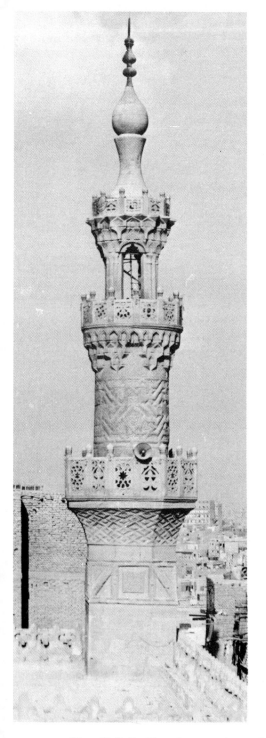

Plate 67 (*left*). The minaret at the *madrasa* of Sultan Qaytbay at Qal'at al-Kabsh

Plate 68 (*right*). The minaret added by Yashbak min Mahdi at the shrine of Imam al-Layth (*photo: Antiquity Department*)

Plate 69 (*above*).   The minaret at the mosque of
Qaytbay at Rawda

Plate 70 (*right*).   The minaret of Azbak al-Yusufi

Plate 71. The minaret of Mughulbay Taz (1468)

Plate 72 (*left*). Tamim al-Rasafi (1471)
Plate 73 (*right*). Timraz al-Ahmadi (1472)

The minaret at the mausoleum of Sultan Qaytbay 879/1474

The minaret of Sultan al-Ashraf Qaytbay in the northern cemetery is worth mentioning not only because of its esthetic value — its carving is exquisite, its proportions ideal — but also because it is a document of special interest.

At the turn of the fifteenth to the sixteenth century, a *mu'adhdhin* spent long hours on the roof of the mosque of Qaytbay (which combined a monastery for Sufis with a college and a mausoleum as well as a Koran school for children) overlooking the panorama of Cairo to the west, the Muqattam hill and the Citadel to the east and south, while to the north he could contemplate the meeting between the gardens of Cairo and the desert. Wherever the shaft of the minaret received enough light from door and window openings, this *mu'adhdhin* would carve long bands of inscriptions in a nice *naskhi* script on the internal walls of the minaret. Some of the exterior parts of the minaret as well as the base of the dome are also adorned with his inscriptions. His name was Muhammad al-Binani, (or possibly al-Tinani) as he several times signed himself, adding the title *al-mu'adhdhin* to his name, as well as different dates, the earliest being 885 (1480) and the latest 911 (1505). As already mentioned, *mu'adhdhin*s were usually educated and were often recruited from among the members of the Sufi community living in the religious building itself, where calligraphy was one of the few activities allowed. (Another, though much earlier example of a *mu'adhdhin* talented at carving inscriptions is the man who in the ninth century carved the inscriptions of the Nilometer, a *mu'adhdhin* at the mosque of 'Amr.) Most of the texts in the minaret of Qaytbay are Koranic, urging believers to remember God and to mention his name, "for He is the Mightiest," but other inscriptions include homilies:

There are four kinds of humiliation: to be poor, to be ill, to have debts...

There are four ways of achieving perfection: by intelligence, by good morals, by piety and...

Death, which you try to escape, will catch you.

Do not fear your enemies, for God is Powerful against them.

I have found more support in long suffering than in men.

God is my love and my succor.

Life is an hour; let it be one of devotion.

Everything is condemned to vanish.

Death must be.

May God have mercy upon him who has carved this.

Know, people, that you will find there should be no confidence.

He who is modest will be appreciated; he who is greedy will be humiliated.

There is no escape from destiny, no rest in this world, no rescue from Death.

God have mercy upon us; You are most Merciful.

Death spares neither father nor son.

Death is the greatest moralist.

How strange he who sheds tears for an eye(?) lost and does not weep for his lack of morals. Even more strange to see so clearly the sins of others with eyes God has struck with blindness. May God forgive the writer and the reader (of this) and our brothers, all the *mu'adhdhin*s; may He forgive their sins. (These words seem to be provoked by another *mu'adhdhin* who, like many, was blind.)

Plates 74a *and* 74b. Inscriptions carved on the interior walls of the minaret of Qaytbay in the cemetery

Plate 75. The minaret of Qaytbay's mausoleum in the cemetery

Plate 76. The minaret of Bardabak (Umm al-Ghulam) (*ca*1475)

Plate 77. Janim al-Bahlawan (1478)

Plate 78. Abu Bakr Muzhir (147

Plate 79. The minaret of Qijmas al-Ishaqi (1481)

The minaret of Abu'l-'Ila ca890/1485

Though this is a construction of the usual Qaytbay style aready described, it deserves special attention because of its inscription bands, the most extensive in Cairo. They run around the shaft of the minaret, two of them on the lower part and the upper parts of the octagonal first story, and quote together from one single *Sura* of the Koran, while four rectangular panels between the small balconies are inscribed with verses from the same *Sura*. Eighteen verses altogether, from the beginning of *Sura* LXVII, are inscribed on the minaret.

In most cases when a minaret carries more than one inscription band, each band contains a fragment from a different *Sura*. The devotion of both bands here to a single *Sura* is thus an unusual feature, as are the inscribed rectangular panels, as well as the square Kufic panels in the transitional zone. The text of *Sura* LXVII, *Surat al-Mulk,* is full of mystic lyricism and symbolism. It deals with the miracle of creation, stresses the contrast between the divine mysteries of the universe and man's perception of them. It warns unbelievers. The choice of this Koranic text in particular, which belongs to the late Meccan *Sura*s, was probably not haphazard, since it is the only time this text is used in architectural epigraphy in medieval Cairo. The reason for the choice may reside in the life of the Sufi shaikh, Abu'l-'Ila, for whom this mosque was built, described by his biographers as full of miracles and wonders. Shaikh Abu 'Ali, popularly called Abu'l-'Ila, lived in a chapel (*zawiya*) built for him by a sponsor and was buried in the mausoleum adjoining it, of which the dome and the inscribed minaret are the only original fifteenth century structures of the present building.

Among the many wonders attributed to the Shaikh Abu'l-'Ila are his metamorphoses: he sometimes took the form of a lion, sometimes of an elephant; once he became a boy and another time was transformed into a soldier. His habit of grasping earth in his hand and turning it into gold and silver brought him under suspicion of practicing alchemy. Reported to have spent forty years in a doorless cell with only one window, he is also said to have been surrounded by a swarm of mosquitoes wherever he went. He had enemies who decided to get rid of him. They killed him with a sword and dumped his body outside the city, only to find him next morning in the best of health in his chapel and telling them, "the moon must have deceived you!" For the mosque of such a man, whose life was adorned with wondrous anecdotes, the choice of *Surat al-Mulk* is quite appropriate. According to the traveler Ibn Battuta, *Surat al-Mulk* was one of the texts always recited in the rituals of Sufis in Cairo.

The minaret of Abu'l-'Ila was heavily restored by the Comité de conservation des monuments d'art arabe, demolished and rebuilt with the addition of a new top story. During the reconstruction operation the stone blocks of the base were reassembled incorrectly with the result that the square Kufic text cannot be read properly.

Plate 80. The minaret of Abu'l-'ila

The minaret of al-'Alaya at Bulaq ninth/late fifteenth century

Although the *Index* assigns this building to the seventeenth century, its minaret looks like a fine example of Mamluk craftmanship. Its most remarkable feature is the carving that decorates the second story, resembling a porcupine motif that has parallels at the minaret of Amir Husayn (rebuilt in the fifteenth century) and the minaret of al-Khatiri (1336) formerly at Bulaq, as well as the minaret of al-Ashraf Inal (1451/53).

The minaret of al-'Alaya is in brick with a carved stucco facing. The octagonal first story has features dating it between the middle and the second half of the fifteenth century: bunches of triple colonettes at each of the eight corners, carved panels on each of the four sides of the transitional zone, as well as the extensive molding running along the sides of the transitional zone. No such example of craftmanship from the seventeenth century is known.

The mosque of al-'Alaya is mentioned in an endowment deed* as the foundation of Qilij Arslan Sultan of al-'Alaya. 'Alaya or Alanya is the name of the Anatolian port city founded by 'Ala' al-Din Kaykubad** in the early thirteenth century. The city of 'Alaya was sold in 1427 by the Karaman rulers to the Mamluk Sultan al-Ashraf Barsbay. When the Ottomans captured 'Alaya in 1472, it was governed by a descendant of the Rum Saljuk dynasty, Qilij Arslan, son of Lutfi Bey. A son of Qilij Arslan lived in Egypt and died there in 913 (1507).*** Historical details thus confirm the architectural analysis of features of the minaret in question, which must therefore be dated to the late Mamluk period, sometime before 1507.

The minaret of Badr al-Din al-Wana'i 902/1496

This construction exhibits nothing remarkable except the pronounced sloping of its walls, which gives a special character to its silhouette. Minarets with similar sloping walls existed in provincial architecture. The foundation deed of the mosque of Badr al-Din al-Wana'i is dated 902 (1496). (Dar al-Watha'iq al-Qawmiyya No. 221 (35).)

---

* Awqaf Nr 974. Ms. Nelly Hanna drew my attention to this document.
** *Encyclopaedia of Islam* (2), Art. Alanya.
*** I am grateful to Prof. Andreas Tietze for having drawn my attention to this information.

Plate 81 (*left*). The minaret of Khushqadam al-Ahmadi (1486)

Plate 82 (*right*). The minaret of al-'Alaya

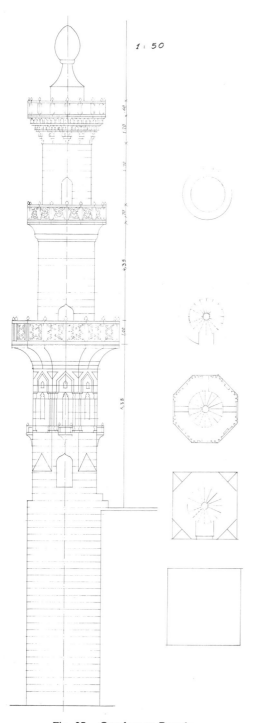

Fig. 27. Qaytbay at Rawda

Plate 83. Badr al-Din al-Wan

The minaret of 'Ali al-Imari ninth-tenth/late fifteenth-early sixteenth century

Assigned in the *Index* (No. 151) to the sixteenth century, this minaret is an attractive construction built in the late Mamluk tradition, with a second story displaying the oft-repeated zig-zag carving. It has one extraordinary feature, however: the stalactites beneath both small balconies of the octagonal section and the first gallery are different from any other Cairene stalactites, with dripping structures of elaborate carved shape. They are not an invention of the craftsman who built the minaret, but have a prototype in Ottoman architecture in Brussa where they exist on buildings of the mid-fourteenth century, and in Istanbul, where from the fifteenth century onward, they decorate minarets and portals.

The mosque of 'Ali al-'Imari is not dated, nor is its sponsor identified. Stylistic comparison suggests the end of the Mamluk period, i.e. the late fifteenth or early sixteenth century. The presence of Ottoman influence on the stalactites, however, is not enough of an argument to attribute the minaret to the Ottoman period, since all mosques built during the two centuries following the Ottoman conquest — with the exception of the mosque of al-Burdayni — had Ottoman minarets.

The minarets of the reign of Sultan al-Ghuri 906-22/1501-16

As already demonstrated, the fashion for three-storied minarets, changing between rectangular, octagonal and circular shape at each level, did not mean the end of the minarets with a rectangular shaft. In the reign of al-Ghuri, three minarets were built with entirely rectangular shafts. Two of them were built by Qanibay al-Rammah, the third one, which is composed of four stories, is the minaret attached to the funerary complex of al-Ghuri. Except for stalactites below the galleries of the *mu'adhdhin* they have almost no decoration. The two minarets of Amir Qanibay al-Rammah, at Nasiriyya (911/1506) and below the Citadel (908/1503) — the latter entirely rebuilt by the Comité — both have at their tops a double-headed structure like the minaret of al-Ghuri at the mosque of al-Azhar. They thus mark the first time since the stone bulb carried on eight columns replaced the *mabkhara* that a change occurs in the upper structure of Cairene minarets, though they are not the earliest examples of the change: al-Jabarti writes that the mosque of Janbalat, once located near Bab al-Nasr, but demolished by the French, used to have a double-headed minaret. Janbalat ruled briefly in 1500.

149

Plate 84a. The minaret of 'Ali al-Imari

Plate 84b. Detail of stalactite carvi
'Ali al-Imari

Fig. 28 (*left*). Al-Ghuri *(Prisse d'Avennes)*

Plate 85 *(right)*. The minaret of Azdumur

The minaret attached to the mausoleum of Sultan al-Ghuri formerly had four bulbs at the top; the present five bulbs are an incorrect modern reconstruction. The four bulbs used to be covered with green tiles, as was the mausoleum dome of the Sultan. Similar tiles decorate the minaret of Sulayman Pasha at the Citadel (1528), as well as the minaret of Shahin al-Khalwati, built a few years later. (The earliest example we know of a minaret decorated with tiles is the minaret of Baybars al-Jashankir (1303-4), which has preserved bits of the original green ceramic tiles.) The minaret of al-Ghuri's mausoleum was not built without problems. Two years after its construction, a deficiency appeared in the masonry, and the original minaret had to be pulled down and rebuilt. Ibn Iyas writes that the top of the minaret had leaned under the heavy weight of the four bulbs. Since they were then rebuilt in brick, the first construction was perhaps all in stone. Tiles were also applied at the minaret of al-Ghuri attached to al-Azhar: here they are blue, cut in the shape of arrows, and inlaid in stone instead of the usual carving.

There is one more minaret in Cairo built by Sultan al-Ghuri, that at 'Arab Yasar (915/1510, Index No. 159), on the western side of the Suyuti cemetery. This minaret, which does not at all look like a royal construction, carries a unique feature, which gives it an awkward appearance: instead of standing above the roof of the mosque, as do all medieval minarets, it flanks its northern corner at street level, its first gallery being at the roof level of the mosque. Small blue balls, of ceramic or glass paste, decorate the loops of the molding which adorns the shaft.

Qurqumas, who built his religious complex in 1507, remained faithful to the tradition of Qaytbay minarets. Khayrbak, an amir of al-Ghuri, who became the first governor of Egypt under Ottoman rule, and whose *madrasa* was erected in 927 (1520), likewise built his minaret in the late Mamluk style.

The minaret of Azdumur, also built in this period, is an elegant though unpretentious construction, connected to the walls of the building with a small arch, a unique device on a minaret. Its staircase starts at ground level, which suggests that the minaret was never attached to the mosque directly. The mosque has disappeared, but a foundation deed (*waqf*) mentions Azdumur's buildings near the aqueduct, including a palace and a stone mausoleum dome as well as a *madrasa* with a minaret. The *waqf* carries the date 908/1502. (Dar al-Watha'iq al-Qawmiyya, No. 234/55 (37).)

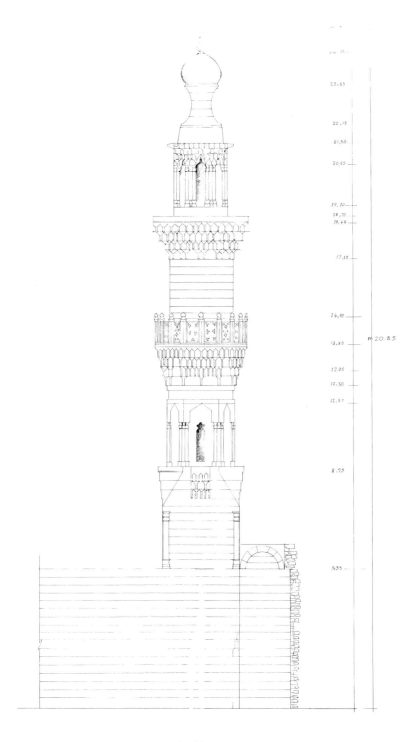

Fig. 29. Azdumur

Plate 86 (*above*). The minaret of
Qanibay al-Rammah below the Citadel,
rebuilt (1503)

Plate 87 (*left*). The minaret at the
madrasa-mausoleum of al-Ghuri (upper
story rebuilt)

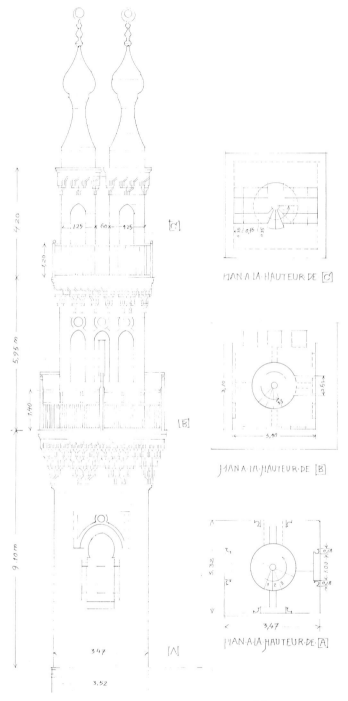

PLAN·A·LA·HAUTEUR·DE [C]

PLAN·A·LA·HAUTEUR·DE [B]

PLAN·A·LA·HAUTEUR·DE·[A]

Fig. 30. Qanibay al-Rammah at Nasiriyya

Plate 88 (*left*). The minaret of Qanibay al-Rammah at Nasiriyya

Plate 89 (*right*). **The minaret at the** complex of Qurqumas

1:100

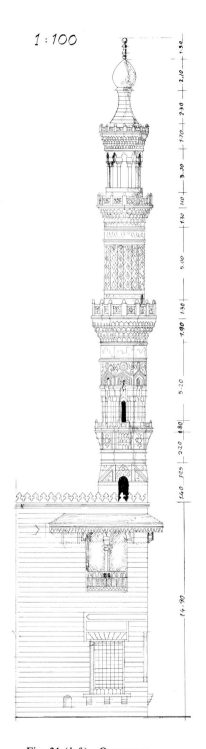

1.30
2.10
2.30
1.70
3.30
1.40 | 1.30
5.00
1.30
7.90 | 1.30
5.20
0.80
2.20
1.40 | 1.05
14.90

Plate 90 *(right)*. The Minaret at the mosque of al-Ghuri at 'Arab Yasar

Fig. 31 *(left)*. Qurqumas

The minaret of Khayrbak at Tabbana 908-927/1502-1520

Khayrbak was a Mamluk amir, the governor of Aleppo during the reign of Sultan al-Ghuri, whose collaboration with the Ottoman conquerors won him the office of the first governor of Ottoman Egypt. His *madrasa* adjoining his mausoleum and his residence at Tabbana are built entirely in the Mamluk style. The mausoleum dome of Khayrbak was erected in 908/1502-3, but the foundation deed of his *madrasa* is dated 927/1520. This means that the college, even if erected slightly earlier than the date of the foundation deed, was founded after the Ottoman conquest, when Khayrbak had become governor. The minaret is not dated. It could have been erected at the same time as the mausoleum dome — a minaret attached to a tomb was no exception — or together with the *madrasa*. The plan of the *madrasa* is very irregular, even by the late Mamluk standards — it had to be squeezed between the existing structures of the palace and the mausoleum — and the attribution of the minaret either to it or to the mausoleum remains quite problematic. In any case, it is the last Mamluk minaret built in Cairo. Under the next Ottoman governors and other sponsors of religious buildings, the minarets of Cairo acquire an Ottoman character.

The minaret of Sulayman Pasha 935/1528

One of the earliest major mosques to be built in Cairo under the Ottoman rule was that of Sulayman Pasha within the Citadel. Its plan is entirely Ottoman, and its minaret follows the style of Istanbul: a cylinder with a conical top. Despite this fact, it displays a typical Mamluk feature: it is adorned with two galleries on stalactites, each story with a different stalactite pattern. Most Ottoman minarets in Cairo, which are in general rather squat towers, have only one gallery.

The pointed cap of the minaret is covered with green tiles, as were the domes surrounding the courtyard of the mosque and that of the prayer hall. These tiles were most probably produced in the workshop responsible for the tiles that once covered the mausoleum dome and the bulbs on the minaret of Sultan al-Ghuri and for the tiles at the top of the minaret of Shahin al-Khalwati.

158

91 (*left*). The minaret at the *madrasa*
ayrbak

92 (*right*). The minaret at the mosque of
man Pasha

Plate 93 (*above left*). The minaret at the mo
of Shahin al Khalwati, with traces of tiles a
top (1538)

Plate 94 (*right*). The minaret at the mosqu
Mahmud Pasha below the Citadel (1568)

Plate 95 (*left*). The minaret at the mosqu
Sinan Pasha at Bulaq (1571)

ate 96. The minaret at the mosque
Masih Pasha (1575)

Plate 97. The minaret at the mosque
of al-Burdayni

The minaret of al-Burdayni 1138/1629

Minarets were usually among the last structures to be added to the construction of
a mosque; in the case of al-Burdayni, however, there is an unusually great gap of
thirteen years between the foundation of the mosque (dated 1105/1616) and that
of the minaret (dated 1138/1629). It is possible, as often happened, that the
original minaret after a while started leaning and had to be replaced by a new
structure. This minaret, like the mosque to which it is attached, is a nostalgic
attempt to revive the architectural art of the Qaytbay period: it has an octagonal
first story with a gallery on stalactites; its middle section is carved. The bulb,
however, rests directly on the second story, without the intermediary of the
columns used in the Mamluk period. Yet both the quality of its carving and the
proportions of this minaret remain below the standard of the Qaytbay period.
This example demonstrates that once certain techniques and canons, like those
which set architectural proportions, are abandoned, it is difficult to make a good
copy of previous models.

Shaikh al-Burdayni was a *qadi* of the Shafiʻi rite and came from an old family of Egyptian jurists. The Ottomans adhered to the Hanafi rite, but never tried to impose it upon the Egyptian population whose majority was Shafiʻi, therefore the post of Shaikh al-Azhar remained throughout the Ottoman period in the hands of Shafiʻi *qadi*s. The style of al-Burdayni's minaret is Egyptian, unlike most of the contemporary ones built in the Turkish style. It is possible that Shaikh al-Burdayni, being Egyptian and moreover a Shafiʻi judge, meant to have his mosque and particularly its minaret built and decorated according to local tradition. This is the only Ottoman minaret in Cairo to carry an inscription; it is historical, and includes the name of the sponsor and the date of construction.

The minaret at the mosque of Amir Ulmas 1125/1713

Examined in comparison with the attractive mosque to which it is attached, (built in 730/1330 by the powerful and wealthy Amir Ulmas), the minaret does seem not to fit stylistically at all. The honeycomb-like stalactites below its single gallery do not resemble any other stalactites of the Mamluk period, and it has almost no decoration. There is an inscription band running around the lower part of the octagonal section, in which, although the name Ulmas can be identified, the rest of the text is illegible. The inscribed stone blocks look dislocated. Hasan ʻAbd al-Wahhab has attributed this minaret to an Ottoman restoration, basing his statement on stylistic arguments. This attribution can be confirmed by historical sources as well, which report that the original minaret of Ulmas collapsed in the year 1125/1713 and was immediately rebuilt, re-using the same stones: hence undoubtedly the illegible inscription band (see al-Jalabi, p. **705**).

The smaller minaret at the mosque of Sultan Hasan (1660) is another attempt in Ottoman Cairo to build a minaret in the late Mamluk style. A glance at the southeastern facade of the mausoleum is sufficient to demonstrate the decline of craftmanship at that time (see plate 39).

The minaret of Muhammad Bey Abu'l-Dhahab 1188/1774

This minaret attached to the mosque located opposite al-Azhar is unique for this period: it is totally rectangular and built in three stories. Atop the third story a structure composed of five jars crowns the minaret. It is a close imitation of the minaret of al-Ghuri located a few steps away. The return to a Mamluk model, displayed at this minaret, may have a political interpretation: Abu'l-Dhahab was a Mamluk of Amir ʻAli Bey al-Kabir who rebelled against the Ottomans and tried to make Egypt and Syria independent under his rule. Abu'l-Dhahab, who had first

162

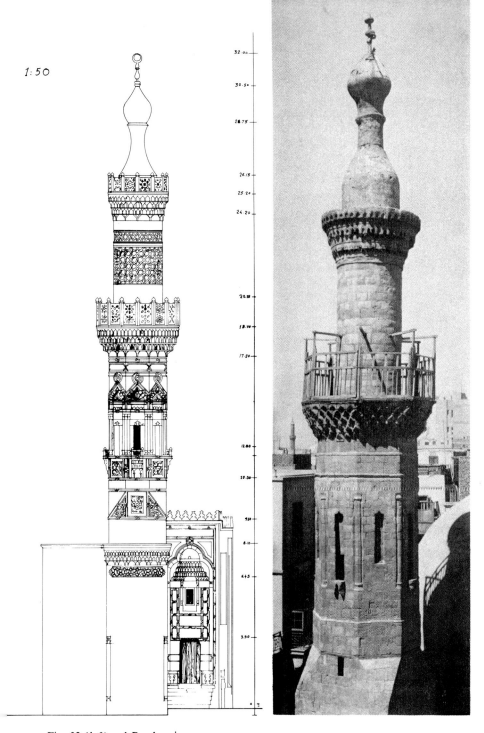

1:50

Fig. 32 (*left*). al-Burdayni

Plate 98 (*right*). The minaret added at the mosque of Ulmas in 1713

Plate 99. The minaret at the mosque of al-Kurdi (1732)

Plate 100. The minaret at the mos: of Abu'l-Dhahab

Plate 101 (*left*).   The minaret of Hasan Pasha
Tahir

Plate 102 (*right*).   The minaret of Sulayman Agha
al-Silahdar at the Coppersmiths'

Plate 103. The minaret of Muhammad ‘Ali

joined 'Ali Bey's rebellion, later turned against his master and tried to assume supremacy. His minaret, reviving the memory of al-Ghuri, who had died fighting the Ottomans, may symbolize emancipation from Ottoman hegemony, which for centuries had also dictated the style of the skyline of Cairo.

The minaret of Hasan Pasha Tahir 1224/1809

After the minaret of Abu'l-Dhahab, another was built in the Mamluk style, the minaret of Hasan Pasha Tahir. This one follows the classical pattern: it is built with three stories, each having a balcony on stalactites. The third story, although it has the shape of Mamluk minaret tops, is solid as is always the case in minarets of the Ottoman period. The tall shaft is lavishly carved, an exception at this period, imitating Mamluk decoration.

The minarets of Muhammad 'Ali 1265/1848

Towards the end of the Ottoman period, Cairene architecture began to reflect the style of Istanbul more deeply than ever before. Until the close of the eighteenth century, architecture in Cairo had remained Mamluk with some Ottoman influence. With the reign of Muhammad 'Ali came a new tendency to break with local traditions. Paradoxically enough, this break was happening not only at a time when Egypt was emancipating itself from Ottoman hegemony but also at a time when the style of Istanbul itself was very much influenced by European art. It may have been this fact that made the Istanbul style of architecture attractive to the new rulers of Egypt, who were very eager to introduce European modernism.

Muhammad 'Ali's concern with independence from the Ottoman sultan was coupled with a determination to eliminate once for all Mamluk power in Egypt. His mosque at the Citadel (1848), deliberately erected on the site of the palace that for centuries had been the residence of the Mamluk sultans, is purely Ottoman, not only in its plan, but also in its decoration, without one of those traces of Mamluk architectural decoration that had typified all Ottoman buildings hitherto. Built in the style of Istanbul, it reflects the regal ambitions of its sponsor, which reached far beyond those of a mere provincial governor, while at the same time demonstrating the total abandonment, without any concessions, of Mamluk traditions. It thus clearly expresses Muhammad 'Ali's politics.

Because of its prestigious location and high visibility, the mosque of Muhammad 'Ali came to be the landmark of the city of Cairo, though it is the least Egyptian of all Cairene mosques. For the uninstructed, it therefore came to represent traditional architecture in its most impressive form! Its dual minarets are the only ones of Ottoman Cairo that could stand comparison with the minarets of Istanbul. They are an architectural tour de force: eighty-three meters high, standing on a rectangular base that measures only three meters on a side. While the spherical silhouette of the mosque itself dominates the skyline of the old city with its cascade of domes, the slender verticality of its minarets cuts the soft horizontal lines of the Muqattam hill and the stretch of sky behind with sharp contrast.

The minaret of al-Rifaʻi 1330/1911

By the end of the nineteenth century, the taste for Mamluk revived — curiously enough, but quite typically — under the influence of European architects and cultural advisers, who were themselves influenced by European orientalism. The mosque of al-Rifaʻi (1911), designed by the Egyptian architect Husayn Pasha Fahmi and completed by the Austrian Herz Bey, is the best example of this revival. Its portal is surmounted by a pair of minarets that imitate the minaret of Asanbugha, while the building itself has deceived many tourists into thinking it contemporary with the mosque of Sultan Hasan, nearly six centuries older, which faces it across the street.

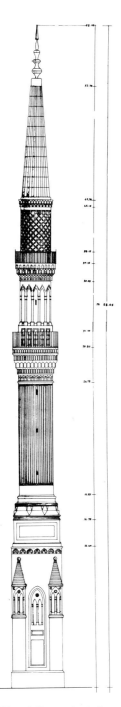

Fig. 33. al-Husayn's shrine

Plate 104. The minaret at the
shrine of al-Husayn

Lost minarets

It will never be known for certain how many medieval constructions have disappeared with time. Engravings and photographs by European travellers in nineteenth century Cairo, however, have preserved the memory of a few buildings that no longer exist. Among these are minarets of great archeological interest, in particular those once attached to buildings which still stand.

A mabkhara minaret depicted by Coste

Among the most spectacular illustrations made by Coste, the French architect of Muhammad 'Ali, is that of a minaret of the *mabkhara* type said to be located in the cemetery of Sayyida Nafisa. No further information concerning the identity of the building is given so that we are left only with stylistic analysis and topographical research.

At first glance, this minaret immediately recalls the minaret of al-Salih Najm al-Din Ayyub. Its *mabkhara* top is almost identical with that of al-Salih, except that it is perhaps more slender. Its rectangular shaft is decorated with a series of medallions and keel-arched panels similar to the arrangement of the minaret at the shrine of al-Husayn and a number of other early Mamluk minarets. The construction is brick and the scale shown in the illustration very much suggests that it must have belonged to a royal construction.

The wife of Sultan al-Salih Najm al-Din Ayyub, the famous Shajar al-Durr, who after her husband's death became sultan for three months, is reported in historical sources to have erected a complex in the cemetery of Sayyida Nafisa, including a *madrasa,* a mausoleum, a palace, a bath and gardens. Today only her mausoleum dome (1250) has survived, but a minaret is reported to have existed until 1877, when it was torn down to make way for a new mosque. At that time, around forty years after Coste made his illustration, it must have already been dilapidated. In any case it could very well have been this minaret that impressed Coste sufficiently to make him choose to illustrate it in his documentation of the great Islamic monuments in Cairo.

The minaret of al-Zahir Baybars· 667/1269

The mosque of al-Zahir Baybars, one of the largest and most impressive buildings of medieval Cairo, has no remaining minaret. Though it is very dilapidated today, its general proportions, particularly the size of the dome that formerly stood over

170

Plate 105. A *mabkhara* minaret depicted last century by Coste

the prayer hall as large as the dome of Imam Shaf'i, still give an idea of the magnificence it must once have displayed. It was built in the tradition of the mosque of al-Hakim and has three monumental entrances, two smaller portals in addition to the main entrance on the axis of the prayer niche.

When Bonaparte's troops occupied Cairo, they found the mosque of Baybars long abandoned and minus many of its columns. Attracted by its location and its thick walls, the French turned it into a fortress, which they named Fort Schulkowsky after one of Bonaparte's officers who had been killed by the rebellious population of the Husayniyya quarter in which the mosque is located. Al-Jabarti writes that the French installed a cannon on the roof of the mosque and used its sole extant minaret as a watchtower. An illustration in the *Description de l'Egypte* shows the stub of the minaret, a rectangular shaft with keel-arched panels similar to that of al-Salih Najm al-Din and early Mamluk minarets, over the main entrance. Like the surviving examples of this period, it probably had a *mabkhara* top. Evliya Celebi, who lived in Egypt in the seventeenth century, reports that the mosque of Baybars had three short (i.e. topless) minarets, but does not indicate their location. If there were three, then most probably the other two were located over the side portals. It is very likely, indeed, that the large mosque of Baybars did have more than one minaret, because when it was built it was outside the urban center of Cairo in a northern suburb beyond Bab al-Futuh. The minaret on the axis of the prayer hall would not have been visible nor the *adhan* from it audible to the townsfolk. A minaret over the side entrance on the southwestern wall would have been visible, however, and the call to prayer could have been heard more clearly. The location of the mosque may be, among others, a reason for the huge dome having been built over the prayer hall. It is a massive back wall that faces the city, and the effect of the dome set above this wall, flanked by the salients at its corners, would have made the view of the building from the city spectacular. The staircase that leads to the roof and to the minarets is contained in the western salient.

The minaret in Bab al-Wazir

Another example of a lost minaret was photographed by Frith in the last century (around 1857). Identifying the location of this building presents no problem: it is clear from the picture that the minaret stood in Shari' Bab al-Wazir, a couple of houses north of the mosque of Aytimish al-Bajasi (whose unique stone dome is visible in the foreground on the right side of the picture), and south of the palace built by Alin Aq that became later the palace of Khayrbak, which is visible in the background. Near the minaret on its northern side, one can make out a structure that looks like a trilobe portal. The minaret photographed by Frith is very similar

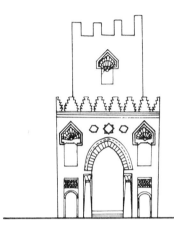

Fig. 34. al-Zahir Baybars (stub)

Plate 106. A minaret at the Bab al-Wazir Street, photographed last century by Frith

to the minaret of **Baybars al-Jashankir** (1309), the unique extant example of a *mabkhara* minaret with a circular middle shaft: its ribbed helmet likewise rests on a circular shaft, but unlike the minaret of Baybars al-Jashankir, it is built in two stories, so that only two (instead of three) rows of stalactites adorn its shaft. The lower stalactites that border the square shaft resemble those of both Baybars al-Jashankir and al-Nasir Muhammad (1309). There is enough stylistic evidence to attribute this lost minaret to the early fourteenth century, i.e. the reign of al-Nasir Muhammad. It is probably this building that 'Ali Mubarak identifies as the "mosque of Bab al-Wazir" and attributes mistakenly to Qusun.

Apart from this stylistic comparison that assigns the minaret on the photograph by Frith to the early fourteenth century, a historic reference may offer a clue to more accurate identification. Ibn Iyas in his report on the plunder of the house of Aytimish al-Bajasi mentions that the dome of a daughter of Sultan al-Nasir Muhammad, Khawand Zahra, was located in the same neighborhood as Aytimish's house. This house of Aytimish, as a matter of fact, was the palace built in the late fourteenth century by Alin Aq, as can be deduced from the foundation document of Aytimish. Its ruins form the foreground landmark on our photograph. If the foundation of Khawand Zahra was located near Aytimish's house it may well have been the building to which the minaret on Frith's photograph was attached. Khawand Zahra's foundation must have been built sometime during the fourteenth century, as is the case with the minaret in question. Both the location of Khawand Zahra's structure by Ibn Iyas* and the style of the minaret on Frith's photograph suggest the probability that this was the minaret of Khawand Zahra. This identification is strengthened by the foundation deed of Amir Khayrbak which indicates a waterwheel belonging to Khawand Zahra among the boundaries of the Alin Aq palace (later also residence of Khayrbak).

---

* Ms Layla 'Ali Ibrahim has drawn my attention to this information: Ibn Iyas I(2) p. 560, Maqrizi, *Suluk* II(3) p. 840. Also the *waqf* of Khayrbak "Dar al-Watha'iq al-Qawmiyya," dated 927H Nr 292(44).

Plate 107 An early Mamluk mabkhara on a 19th-century photograph (probably at the shrine of Sulayman al-Rifaʻi at Suwayqat al-ʻIzzi

An early Mamluk mabkhara minaret

Another example of a *mabkhara* type minaret of the early Mamluk period is just visible in a photographic panorama taken from Bab al-Wazir, with the palace of Alin Aq and the mosque of Khayrbak to the right and the mosque of Sultan Hasan dominating the background. In the middle of the panorama is a minaret consisting of a square shaft adorned with four medallions; above the square shaft is a structure resembling the upper part added by Baybars al-Jashankir to the minarets of al-Hakim. It looks dilapidated, and its upper portion is partly missing. This minaret must have collapsed shortly after the photograph was taken. Stylistically, it belongs to the early Mamluk period. Its location seems to correspond with that of the *ribat* (Sufi foundation) of Sulayman al-Rifaʻi, of which only a dome has survived dated 697 (1297), a date that could very well be that of this minaret.

175

Plate 108 (*right*). The minaret of the mosq
of al-Khatiri

The minaret of al-Khatiri 734/1336

This minaret, which is listed in the *Index* (No 341), was destroyed in the 1960's. Nothing of the original building, located in the river-side quarter of Bulaq, has survived. A photograph shows the minaret as a brick construction with carved stucco decoration in a porcupine motif similar to that of Amir Husayn, Inal and al-'Alaya.

Two minarets in the northern cemetery

An illustration in the *Description de l'Egypte* of a part of the northern cemetery near the mausoleum of Barquq shows two minarets which have now disappeared. The minaret on the right in the illustration is almost identical with that of al-Baqli and is very similar to that of Fatima Khatun. A doorway in the lower part of the shaft indicates that it was probably free-standing. Double-light windows with what seem to be horseshoe arches are set in the two visible sides of its square shaft.
 The dome shown to the left of this minaret, which does not belong to the same period, is part of the mausoleum of Amir 'Asfur (1506), located on the western side of the Barquq complex. The other minaret, on the left of the illustration, resembles the northern minaret at the mosque of al-Nasir Muhammad at the Citadel, which today has no parallel. It is of the square-circular type with a balcony in the square part.

te 109. Two minarets in the northern cemetery depicted in the *Description d'Egypte*

The minaret of the Barmawiyya mosque ninth/fifteenth century

This minaret stub was depicted last century by Hay. Its style assigns it to the mid-fifteenth century. The mosque, which still stands near Bab al-Bahr Street, has been completely rebuilt. Maqrizi mentions a shaikh called Muhammad 'Abd al-Dayim al-Barmawi who in the first quarter of the fifteenth century used to teach at the mosque of al-Fakhri. He could well be the person who sponsored the mosque to which this minaret was attached.

Plate 110. A minaret stub at the Barmawiyya mosque depicted last century by Hay

The minaret of Shaikh Muhammad al-Ghamri   *ca843/1439*

A minaret beautifully illustrated by Roberts is that once attached to the mosque of
Shaikh Muhammad al-Ghamri on the Marjush street in the old city center. When
depicted by Roberts, the minaret was in excellent shape. It was destroyed by the
Comité de conservation des monuments d'art arabe last century after the whole
construction had decayed to the point of collapse.

Plate 111. The minaret of Shaikh Muhammad al-Ghamri depicted last century by Roberts

The minaret of Qanim al-Tajir (al-Qalmi) 871/1466

A drawing by Prisse d'Avennes illustrates a minaret without a top, its middle section carved with the same pattern as the minaret of Asanbugha and some later ones. The artist attributes the minaret to "al-Kalmy," without further indication. On the Cairo map of the *Description de l'Egypte* (map reference X10-196) the mosque of "al-Qalmy" is located near the mosque of Ibn Tulun in the same place indicated on the Grand Bey plan of 1874 as the mosque of "al-Tagher" (*Index* No 222). The foundation deed of the mosque, also mentioned by 'Ali Mubarak, is dated 871/1466; it belongs to Amir Qanim al-Sharkasi al-Tajir, a Mamluk of Sultan al-Mu'ayyad Shaikh.

ate 112 (*left*). The minaret of Sultan Jaqmaq at
ayr al-Nahas (see p. 128)

g. 35 (*right*). Qanim al-Tajir (*Prisse d'Avennes*)

Plate 113. The minaret of Sultan Qansuh Abu Sa'id

The minaret of Sultan Qansuh Abu Sa'id (904/1499

This minaret can be seen in a view of the northern cemetery depicted at the beginning of the nineteenth century by Coste. It shows on the left the religious-funerary complexes of Amir Qurqumas and Sultan Inal, while to the right the mausoleum of Sultan Qansuh Abu Sa'id can be identified. Next to the dome is the rectangular shaft of a topless minaret which seems to have belonged to a funerary complex, of which only the dome survives today.

The rectangular type of minaret was revived in the late Mamluk period, especially during the reign of Sultan al-Ghuri in the early sixteenth century.

The minaret of Sultan al-'Adil Tumanbay 906/1501

Sultan al-'Adil Tumanbay built a large religious complex, which included a mosque and his mausoleum, as well as several residential structures, on the caravan road to Sinai. Today, a lonely dome has survived within the military barracks on the road to Heliopolis. A nineteenth century drawing shows the remains of the mosque as well as its minaret, which appears to be typical of the late Mamluk period. The mosque was destroyed in the last century by Ibrahim Pasha to make place for a paper factory.

184

Fig. 36. Sultan al-‘Adil Tumanbay (*Owen Jones*)

The adhan: the call to prayer

by Layla Ali Ibrahim

The use of the call to prayer began in Madina one year after the Hijra, when the Muslim community was first beginning to take shape. Early Arab historians relate that the Prophet Muhammad asked his companions to establish a call to prayer that would differ from that of the Christians and the Jews. Together they decided that the Muslim call to prayer, the *adhan,* should consist of the human voice, and would be performed by a person known as a "mu'adhdhin." Although the *adhan* is performed exclusively before the obligatory five daily prayers, it has a different status from the actual prayers. The call to prayer is *sunna,* i.e. it is recommended not obligatory (*fard*). Of the four orthodox rites, it is only the Hanbali who claim that the *adhan* is a *fard kifaya;* that is, obligatory on a Muslim community, but not on the entirety of the population as long as someone in the community performs it.

The Prophet and his companions chose Bilal, a freed slave of Abu Bakr, as the first *mu'adhdhin.* He performed the call to prayer during the lifetime of the Prophet and during the caliphate of Abu Bakr.

There is no fixed melody for the *adhan;* on the contrary the *'ulama*s (theologians) disapprove of it. Egypt, however, has always had a particular melody which is still used in the *adhan* today.

The traditional Sunni *adhan* consists of seven phrases, with two additional ones for the morning prayer:

1. *Allahu Akbar* (Allah is most great) intoned four times. This phrase is called *al-takbir.*

2. *Ashhadu anna la ilah ill'-Allah* (I testify that there is no god besides Allah) intoned twice.

3. *Ashhadu anna Muhammadan rasul Allah* (I testify that Muhammad is the apostle of Allah) intoned twice. Phrases two and three are called the *shihada* (confession of faith).

4. *Hayya 'ala 'l-salah* (Come to prayer) intoned twice.

5. *Hayya 'ala 'l-falah* (Come to salvation) intoned twice. Phrases four and five are called *tathwib.*

6. *Allahu Akbar* (Allah is most great) intoned twice.

187

7. *La ilah ill'-Allah* (There is no god besides Allah) intoned once.

The two additions to the morning prayer of:

Al-salatu khayr min al-nawm (Prayer is better than sleep) intoned twice between the fifth and sixth phrases, and
Al-salatu wa'l-salam 'alayka ya rasul Allah (Benediction and peace upon you, 0 Apostle of Allah) intoned once at the end of the morning prayer by the Hanafis, one of the four Sunni rites.

The differences in the *adhan* of the four Sunni rites lay merely in the repetition of the phrases. The *adhan*s of the Sunni and the Shi'i sects diverge more sharply, however, due to the addition of the phrase, *hayy 'ala khayr al-'amal* (come to the best of work), inserted between the fifth and the sixth phrases of the Shi'i *adhan*. (The complete Shi'i formula, *hayy 'ala khayr al-'amal, Muhammad wa 'Ali khayr al-bashar* (come to the best of work, Muhammad and 'Ali are the best of people), was used in Syria but never in Egypt.)

From the accounts of Arab historians, one infers that the *adhan*, though primarily a call to prayer, also had an important political significance. The extra phrases added to the *adhan* changed with every new regime. When the Fatimids conquered Egypt, they introduced the Shi'i formula, "come to the best of work" between the fifth and sixth phrases. According to Maqrizi, the first time the Shi'i *adhan* was announced in Egypt was on the 8th of Jumada I (359/970) when Jawhar al-Siqilli, the Fatimid general, went to the Friday prayer at the mosque of Ibn Tulun. On the following Friday, it was pronounced at the 'Amr mosque. The mosques nearby later followed suit.

The second addition to the morning prayer was started by Bilal, the *mu'adhdhin* of the Prophet, who said, *al-salat wa'l-salam 'alayka ya Rasul Allah wa rahmat Allah wa barakatuh* (Benediction and peace on you, O Apostle of Allah, and the mercy of Allah and his blessing). Abu Bakr, the first caliph after the Prophet, was mentioned in a similar manner, but as *khalifat Rasul Allah* (Caliph of the apostle of Allah). 'Umar and the caliphs after him were addressed as *amir al-mu'minin* (commander of the faithful). After having established a Shi'i caliphate in Egypt, the Fatimids were addressed in the same way for the morning prayer inside their palace.

The Isma'ili Shi'i Fatimids introduced in the *adhan* the formula *hayy 'ala khayr al-'amal* (come to the best of work), which, as mentioned earlier, was particular to them. The Fatimid caliph al-Hakim abolished this formula for a while, but it was reinstated again after his death. In 524/1130 the Fatimid vizir Abu 'Ali, grandson of Badr al-Jamali and a fanatic Imami Shi'i, ordered that the

Isma'ili Fatimid phrase and the name of Isma'il ibn Ja'far should be omitted from the *adhan* altogether. Two years later Abu 'Ali was murdered, and the Isma'ili *adhan* was reinstated.

Of course, the Shi'i formulation was stopped when Salah al-Din restored Sunnism in Egypt, as Nur al-Din had previously done in Syria. Although Mecca was attached politically to Egypt, the Shi'i Zaydiyya of South Arabia were still very influential and the use of the Shi'i *adhan* continued until 702/1302. At this point in time the Amir Burulji, who was sent to Mecca by al-Nasir Muhammad as Amir al-Hajj (Commander of the Pilgrimage), stopped this practice and reintroduced the Sunni *adhan*.

In the additions to the morning prayer, the title of the appointed governor or ruler of a Muslim province was usually mentioned after that of the caliph. When Salah al-Din assumed sovereign power in Egypt, he had not yet received a diploma of investiture from the 'Abbasid caliph in Baghdad. Consequently, neither his name nor that of the caliph was mentioned during the morning *adhan*. This practice, once established, was continued even after Salah al-Din got his diploma and also throughout the Ayyubid period and into the early Mamluk period, and the morning prayer ended with *al-salam 'alayka ya rasul Allah* (Peace on you, 0 Apostle of Allah). The *muhtasib* of Cairo added the latter phrase to the Thursday evening *adhan* in 760/1359. Later, in 791/1389, during the reign of Sultan Hajji, a Sufi, having seen the Prophet in a dream, suggested to the *muhtasib* of Cairo the addition of the same phrase to every *adhan*. But the classical *adhan*, without this last clause, was restored, and since then the *adhan* has not changed in Egypt.

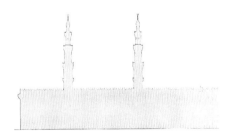

Koranic Epigraphy of Cairene Minarets

Reading the inscriptions carved on medieval minarets is a difficult task because of the dilapidated condition of most of the inscriptions as well as the problem of gaining access to a good view-point. My aim has therefore been limited to identifying the Koranic text, without checking every letter of the inscription. Words missing or abbreviated, or possible mistakes by the craftsman, are not recorded in this survey.

Certain passages from the Koran are used repeatedly in inscriptions. To avoid unnecessary repetition in the text, the four longest of these are printed in full at the beginning, with their references, but are identified by reference only under the individual minarets. The English version used is that by M. Pickthall.

II, 255

Allah! There is no God save Him, the Alive, the Eternal. Neither slumber nor sleep overtaketh Him. Unto Him belongeth whatsoever is in the heavens and whatsoever is in the earth. Who is he that intercedeth with Him save by His leave? He knoweth that which is in front of them and that which is behind them, while they encompass nothing of His knowledge save what He will. His Throne includeth the heavens and the earth, and He is never weary of preserving them. He is the Sublime, the Tremendous.

III, 190-91

Lo! In the creation of the heavens and the earth and (in) the difference of night and day are tokens (of His Sovereignty) for men of understanding, such as remember Allah, standing, sitting, and reclining, and consider the creation of the heavens and the earth, (and say): Our Lord! Thou createdst not this in vain. Glory be to Thee! Preserve us from the doom of Fire.

XXIV, 35

Allah is the Light of the heavens and the earth. The similitude of His light is as a niche wherein is a lamp. The lamp is in a glass. The glass is as it were a shining star. (This lamp is) kindled from a blessed tree, an olive neither of the East nor of the West, whose oil would almost glow forth (of itself) though no fire touched it. Light upon light. Allah guideth unto His light those whom He will. And Allah speaketh to mankind in allegories, for Allah is Knower of all things.

XXIV, 36-8

(This lamp is found) in houses which Allah hath allowed to be exalted and that His name shall be remembered therein. Therein do offer praise to Him at morn and evening men whom neither merchandise nor sale beguileth from

remembrance of Allah and constancy in prayer and paying to the poor their due; who fear a day when hearts and eyeballs will be overturned; that Allah may reward them with the best of what they did, and increase reward for them of His bounty. Allah giveth blessings without stint to whom He will.

The Mosque of Al-Hakim
    a. The Northern Minaret   Upper band XXIV, 35
                                                           XXIV, 36-38
                                                               Middle band V, 55
Your friend can be only Allah; and His messenger and those who believe, who establish worship and pay the poor-due, and bow down (in prayer).
                                                              Lower band IX, 128
There hath come unto you a messenger, (one) of yourselves, unto whom aught that ye are overburdened is grievous, full of concern for you, for the believers full of pity, merciful.
                                                           Stair entrance XVII, 80
And say: My Lord! Cause me to come in with a firm incoming and to go out with a firm outgoing. And give me from Thy presence a sustaining Power.
                                                 Northern upper cube
                             (added by Baybars al-Jashankir) II, 255
    b. The Southwestern Minaret   Middle band XI, 73
The mercy of Allah and His blessings be upon you, 0 people of the house! Lo! He is Owner of Praise, Owner of Glory!
                                                             Lower band, IX, 18
He only shall tend Allah's sanctuaries who believeth in Allah and the Last Day and observeth proper worship and payeth the poor-due and feareth none save Allah. For such (only) is it possible that they can be of the rightly guided.

The Minaret of Sanjar al-Jawli   XXIV, 36-37

The Minaret of Bashtak   Upper band, II, 255
                                                            Lower band, VII, 54
Lo! your Lord is Allah Who created the heavens and the earth in six Days, then mounted He the Throne. He covereth the night with the day, which is in haste to follow it, and hath made the sun and the moon and the stars subservient by His command. His verily is all creation and commandment. Blessed be Allah, the Lord of the Worlds!

The Minaret of Qusun   The top, XXIV, 36-37
                                                   Third story band, XXXIII, 45
0 Prophet! Lo! We have sent thee as a witness and a bringer of good tidings and a warner.

Second story band, IX, 18

He only shall tend Allah's sanctuaries who believeth in Allah and the Last Day and observeth proper worship and payeth the poor-due and feareth none save Allah. For such (only) is it possible that they can be of the rightly guided.

XXXIII, 41-44

O ye who believe! Remember Allah with much remembrance. And glorify Him early and late. He it is Who blesseth you, and His angels (bless you), that He may bring you forth from darkness unto light; and He is ever Merciful to the believers. Their salutation on the day when they shall meet Him will be: Peace. And He hath prepared for them a goodly recompense.

First story, II, 277

Lo! those who believe and do good works and establish worship and pay the poor-due, their reward is with their Lord and there shall no fear come upon them neither shall they grieve.

XXII, 41

Those who, if We give them power in the land, establish worship and pay the poor-due and enjoin kindness and forbid iniquity. And Allah's is the sequel of events.

The Minaret of Aydumur al-Bahlawan   Upper band, III, 190-91

Lo! In the creation of the heavens and the earth and (in) the difference of night and day are tokens (of His Sovereignty) for men of understanding, such as remember Allah, standing, sitting, and reclining, and consider the creation of the heavens and the earth, (and say): Our Lord! Thou createdst not this in vain. Glory be to Thee! Preserve us from the doom of Fire.

Lower band: fragments of prayers

The Minaret of Shaikhu (the mosque)   The neck of the bulb XLVIII, 1

Lo! We have given thee (O Muhammad) a signal victory.

The octagonal section LV, 1-7

The Beneficent hath made known the Qur'ân. He hath created man. He hath taught him utterance. The sun and the moon are made punctual. The stars and the trees adore. And the sky He hath uplifted; and He hath set the measure.

The Minaret of Shaikhu (the monastery)   XXII, 27

And proclaim unto mankind the pilgrimage. They will come unto thee on foot and on every lean camel; they will come from every deep ravine.

The Minaret of Tatar al-Hijaziyya   III, 190-91

The Minaret of Tankizbugha   XXIV, 36-37

193

The "Southern" minaret

Upper band XXIV, 36-37
Lower band, XLI, 30-31

Lo! those who say: Our Lord is Allah, and afterward are upright, the angels descend upon them, saying: Fear not nor grieve, but hear good tidings of the paradise which ye are promised. We are your protecting friends in the life of the world and in the Hereafter. There ye will have (all) that your souls desire, and there ye will have (all) for which ye pray.

The Minaret of the Sultaniyya mausoleum

Upper band III, 190-91
Lower band XXXIII, 41-43

O ye who believe! Remember Allah with much remembrance, and glorify Him early and late. He it is who blesseth you, and His angels (bless you), that He may bring you forth from darkness unto light; and He is Merciful to the believers.

The Minarets of Faraj ibn Barquq

a. The Northern Minaret   LXII, 9

O ye who believe! When the call is heard for the prayer of the day of congregation, haste unto remembrance of Allah and leave your trading. That is better for you if ye did but know.

b. The Southern Minaret   III, 18

Allah (Himself) is Witness that there is no God save Him. And the angels and the men of learning (too are witness). Maintaining His creation in justice, there is no God save Him, the Almighty, the Wise.

The Minaret of Qanibay al-Muhammadi

Upper band, XXIV, 35
Lower band, XXXIX, 73

And those who keep their duty to their Lord are driven unto the Garden in troops till, when they reach it, and the gates thereof are opened, and the warders thereof say unto them: Peace be unto you! Ye are good, so enter ye (the Garden of delight), to dwell therein;

The Minarets of al-Mu'ayyad
a. The Eastern Minaret

Upper band, XXIV, 36-37
Middle band, II, 255
Lower band, XXIV, 36-37

b. The Western Minaret   Upper band, XXXIII, 41-42

O ye who believe! Remember Allah with much remembrance, and glorify Him early and late. He it is who blesseth you, and His angels (bless you), that He may bring you forth from darkness into light; and He is Merciful to the believers.

Middle band, II, 255
Lower band, XXIV, 36-37

The Minaret of Qadi 'Abd al-Basit   XXII, 28

That they may witness things that are of benefit to them, and mention the name of Allah on appointed days over the beast of cattle that He hath bestowed upon them. Then eat thereof and feed therewith the poor unfortunate.

The Minaret of the "madrasa" of Barsbay   LXII, 9

O ye who believe! When the call is heard for the prayer of the day of congregation, haste unto remembrance of Allah and leave your trading. That is better for you if ye did but know.

The Minaret of Kafur al-**Zimam**   XXXIII, 41-42

O ye who believe! Remember Allah with much remembrance, and glorify Him early and late. He it is who blesseth you, and His angels (bless you), that He may bring you forth from darkness into light; and He is Merciful to the believers.

The Minaret of Qanibay al-Sharkasi   II, 255

The Minaret of Qaraqaja al-Hasani   Upper band II, 255
                                  Lower band, VII, 54

Lo! your Lord is Allah Who created the heavens and the earth in six Days, then mounted He the Throne. He covereth the night with the day, which is in haste to follow it, and hath made the sun and the moon and the stars subservient by His command. His verily is all creation and commandment. Blessed be Allah, the Lord of the Worlds!

The Minaret of Qadi Yahya (Azhar Street)   LXII, 9

O ye who believe! When the call is heard for the prayer of the day of congregation, haste unto remembrance of Allah and leave your trading. That is better for you if ye did but know.

The Minaret of Qadi Yahya at Habbaniyya   Upper band, III, 191-192

Such as remember Allah, standing, sitting, and reclining, and consider the creation of the heavens and the earth, (and say): Our Lord! Thou createdst not this in vain. Glory be to Thee! Preserve us from the doom of Fire. Our Lord! Whom Thou causest to enter the Fire: him indeed Thou hast confounded. For evil-doers there will be no helpers.

                                      Lower band, III, 190

Lo! In the creation of the heavens and the earth and (in) the difference of night and day are tokens (of His Sovereignty) for men of understanding.

The Minaret of Qadi Yahya at Bulaq: illegible

The Minaret of Inal

Upper band, II, 255
Lower band, III, 190-191

The Minaret of Tamim al-Rasafi

Upper band, III, 190-191
Lower band, XXXIII, 41-42

O ye who believe! Remember Allah with much remembrance, and glorify Him early and late. He it is who blesseth you, and His angels (bless you), that He may bring you forth from darkness unto light; and He is Merciful to the believers.

The Minaret at the Mausoleum of Qaytbay

Upper band, III, 190-91
Middle band, XXXIII, 41-42

O ye who believe! Remember Allah with much remembrance, and glorify Him early and late. He it is who blesseth you, and His angels (bless you), that He may bring you forth from darkness unto light; and He is Merciful to the believers.

Lower band, LXII, 9

O ye who believe! When the call is heard for the prayer of the day of congregation, haste unto remembrance of Allah and leave your trading. That is better for you if ye did but know.

The Minaret of Yashbak at Imam al-Layth

Upper band, II, 255
Lower band: historical

The Minaret of Shaikh Abu'l-'Ila

Upper band, LXVII, 1-2

Blessed is He in Whose hand is the Sovereignty, and, He is Able to do all things. Who hath created life and death that He may try you which of you is best in conduct; and He is the Mighty, the Forgiving.

Middle band, LXVII, 5-8

And verily We have beautified the world's heaven with lamps, and We have made them missiles for the devils. and for them We have prepared the doom of flame. And for those who disbelieve in their Lord there is the doom of hell, a hapless journey's end! When they are flung therein they hear its roaring as it boileth up, as it would burst with rage. Whenever a (fresh) host is flung therein the wardens thereof ask them: Came there unto you no warner?

Lower band, LXVII, 9-12

They say: Yea, verily, a warner came unto us; but we denied and said: Allah hath naught revealed; ye are in naught but a great error. And they say: Had we been wont to listen or have sense, we had not been among the dwellers in the flames. So they acknowledge their sins; but far removed (from mercy) are the dwellers in the flames. Lo! those who fear their Lord in secret, theirs will

The Northwestern Panel on the socle of the minaret, LXVII, 14-15

Should he not know what He created? And He is the Subtile, the Aware. He it is Who hath made the earth subservient unto you, so walk in the paths thereof and eat of His providence. *And unto Him will be the resurrection (of the dead).*

The Northeastern Panel on the socle, LXVII, 15-16
He it is Who hath made the earth subservient unto you, so walk in the paths thereof and eat of His providence. *And unto Him will be the resurrection (of the dead).* *Have ye taken security from Him Who is in the heaven that He will not cause the earth to swallow you?*

The Northern Panel, LXVII, 17
Or have ye taken security from Him Who is in the heaven that He will not let loose on you a hurricane? *But ye shall know the manner of My warning.*

The Southwestern Panel, LXVII, 18-19
And verily those before them denied, then (see) the manner of My wrath (with them)! *Have they not seen the birds above them spreading out their wings and closing them?* *Naught upholdeth them save the Beneficent.* *Lo! He is Seer of all things.*

The Minaret of Azbak al-Yusufi   Upper band, III, 190-191

The Minaret of Qurqumas   Upper band, II, 255
Middle band, XXXIII, 41-42
O ye who believe! *Remember Allah with much remembrance, and glorify Him early and late.* *He it is who blesseth you, and His angels (bless you), that He may bring you forth from darkness unto light; and He is Merciful to the believers.*
Lower band, XVIII, 108-109
Lo! Those who believe and do good works, theirs are the Gardens of Paradise for welcome, wherein they will abide, with no desire to be removed from thence.

Bibliography

a) Primary sources

'Abd al-Latif al-Baghdadi. *Kitab al-Ifada wa'l I'tibar fi Umur al-Mushahada wa'l Hawadith al-Mu'ayana bi-Ard Misr (Relation de l'Egypte)*, ed. Sylvestre de Sacy. Paris, 1810

Abu Salih. *The Churches and Monasteries of Egypt and some Neighbouring Countries attributed to Abu Salih the Armenian.* ed. & translated B.T.A. Evetts. Oxford, 1895.

al-Ghazzi, Najm al-Din. *al-Kawakib al-Sa'ira bi A'yan al-Mi'a al-'Ashira.* ed. Jibra'il S. Jabbur 3 vols. Bayrut, 1979.

Ibn Battuta. *Tuhfat al-Nuzzar fi Ghara'ib al-Amsar wa 'Aja'ib al-Asfar.* Cairo, 1958.

Ibn al Hajj, al-'Abdari al-Fasi. *al-Madkhal.* 3 vols. Cairo, 1929.

Ibn Iyas, Muhammad Ibn Ahmad. *Bada'i al-Zuhur fi Waqa'i' al-Duhur*, ed. M. Mostafa. Wiesbaden/Cairo, 1963.

Ibn Khaldun, 'Abd al-Rahman. *al-Ta'rif b'Ibn Khaldun wa Rihlatihi Gharban wa Sharqan.* Beyrouth-Cairo, 1979.

Ibn Muyassar, Taj al-Din Muh. Ibn Yusuf Ibn Jalab Raghib *Akhbar Misr* selected by al-Maqrizi, ed. Ayman Fu'ad Sayyid. (Textes arabes et études islamiques, t. XVII.) Le Caire: Institut français d'archéologie orientale, 1981.

Ibn Taghribirdi, Jamal al-Din Abul-Mahasin. *al-Nujum al-Zahira fi Muluk Misr Wa'l-Qahira.* 16 vols. Cairo, 1963-1972.

Ibn Tulun, Shams al-Din Muhammad. *Mufakahat al-Khillan fi Hawadith al-Zaman.* 2 Vols. ed. Muhammad Mustafa. Cairo, 1962-64.

Ibn al-Ukhuwwa, Muhammad b. Ahmad al-Qurashi. Kitab Ma'alim al-Qurba fi Ahkam al-Hisba. ed. M.M. Sha'ban & S. Ahmad 'Isa al-Muti'i. Cairo, 1976.

Ibn Zahira. *al-Fada'il al-Bahira fi Mahasin Misr wa'l-Qahira.* ed. Mustafa al-Saqqa & Kamil al-Muhandis. Cairo, 1969.

al-Jabarti, 'Abd al-Rahman al-Shaykh al-Hanafi. *'Aja'ib al-'Athar fi l-Tarajim wa'l-Akhbar.* 4 vols. Bulaq, 1297 H.

al-Jabali, Ahmad 'Abd al-Ghani. *Awdah al-Isharat fi man wala Misr al-Qahira min al-Wuzara' wa'l-Bashat,* ed. Fu'ad Muhammad al-Mawi. Cairo, 1977.

al-Jawhari, 'Ali ibn Dawud al-Sayrafi. *Nuzhat al-Nufus wa'l-Abdan fi Tawarikh al-Zaman.* 3 vols. Cairo, 1970-1973.

al-Maqrizi, Taqiyy al-Din Ahmad. *Kitab al-Suluk li Ma'rifat Duwwal al-Muluk,* eds. M. Ziyada and A. Ashshur. 4 vols. Cairo, 1934-1973.

al-Maqrizi, Taqiyy al-Din Ahmad. *al-Mawa'iz wa'l-I'tibar fi Dhikr al-Khittat wa'l-Athar.* Bulaq, 1270 H.

Mubarak, 'Ali. *al-Khitat al-Jadida al-Tawfiqiyya li-Misr wa'l-Qahira.* 20 vols. Cairo, 1306 H.

al-Qalqashandi, Abu' l-'Abbas Ahmad ibn 'Ali. *Subh al-A'sha fi Sina'at al-'Insha.* 14 vols. Cairo, 1332-1338 H.

al-Sha'rani, 'Abd al-Wahhab Ibn Ahmad Ibn 'Ali al-Ansari. *al-Tabaqat al-Kubra al-Musammah bi-Lawaqih al-Anwar fi Tabaqat al-Akhyar.* 2 vols. Cairo, 1954.

al-Suyuti, Jalal al-Din 'Abd al-Rahman. *Husn al-Muhadara fi Tarikh Misr wa'l-Qahira.* 2 vols. Cairo, 1968.

al-Warthilani, Sidi Husayn ibn Muhammad. *Nuzhat al-Anzar fi Fadl 'Ilm al-Tarikh wa'l-Akhbar.* Beirut, 1974.

al-Zahiri, Ghars al-Din Khalil ibn Shahin. *Kitab Zubdat Kashf al-Mamalik wa Bayan al-Turuq wa'l-Masalik.* Paris, 1893.

al-Zarakshi, Muhammad Ibn 'Abd Allah. *I'lam al-Sajid bi Ahkam al-Masajid.* Cairo, 1384 ̄ H

b) Secondary Sources

'Abd al-Wahhab, Hasan. *Tarikh al-Masajid al-atariyya.* 2 vols. Cairo, 1946.

'Ali Ibrahim, Layla. "The Transitional Zone of Domes in Cairene Architecture" *Kunst des Orients,* X 1/2 (1975) pp. 5-23.

'Ali Ibrahim, Layla. "The Great Hanqah of the Emir Qawsun in Cairo," with two appendices by J.M. Rogers. *Mitteilungen des Deutschen Archeologische Instituts Abteilung Kairo* 30, 1 (1974), pp. 37-64.

Amin, M. Muhammad. *al-Awqaf wa'l-Hayat al-Ijtima'iyya fi Misr 648-923H/1250-1517.* Cairo,1980.

Asil, Miguel. "The Pharos of Alexandria" (Summary of an essay in Spanish) *Proceedings of the British Academy,* XIX, 1933.

Behrens-Abouseif, Doris. "The last minaret of Shajarat al-Durr at her complex in the cemetery of Sayyida Nafisa", *Mitteilungen des Deutschen Archaeologischen Instituts Abteilung Kairo,* 39 (1983), pp. 1-16.

Bloom, Jonathan. "The mosque of al-Hakim in Cairo," *Muqarnas,* 1 (1983), pp. 15-36.

Bourgoin, J. *Précis de l'Art Arabe.* Paris, 1892.

Bulletin du Comité de Conservation des Monuments de l'Art Arabe. *Procès Verbaux et Rapports.* Cairo, 1882-1953.

Creswell, K.A.C. *A Brief Chronology of the Muhammadan Monuments of Egypt to A.D. 1517.* Cairo, 1919.

Creswell, K.A.C. *The Muslim Architecture of Egypt.* 2 vols. Oxford, 1959.

Creswell, K.A.C. "The Evolution of the Minaret with Special Reference to Egypt." *Burlington Magazine.* March, May, June, 1926.

Description de l'Egypte par les Savants de l'Expedition Française. Etat Moderne. Paris, 1812.

Diez, Ernst. "Manara". *Encyclopaedia of Islam.* 1st. ed. Leyden-London, 1913-1936.

Ebeid, Sophie. *Early Sabils and their Standardization.* M.A. Thesis, American University in Cairo, 1976.

Ettinghausen, Richard. "Hilal". *Encyclopaedia of Islam.* 2nd ed. Leyden, 1960.

Ettinghausen, Richard. "Arabic Epigraphy: Communication or Symbolic Affirmation?" *Studies in Honor of George Miles.* eds. Bacharach, J. and Kouymjian, D.K. Beirut, 1974, pp. 297-317.

Fernandes, Leonor. *The Evolution of the Khanqah Institution in Mamluk Egypt.* Ph.D., Princeton University, 1980.

199

Flury, Samuel. *Die Ornamente der Hakim- Und Ashar- Moschee* Heidelberg, 1912.

Goettlicher, Arvid. *Materialien fuer ein Corpus der Schiffsmodelle im Altertum.* Mainz, 1978.

Gottheil, J.H. "The origin and history of the minaret." *Journal of the American Oriental Society,* XIII (1909-10), pp. 132-54.

El-Hawary, Hassan Mohammad. "Trois Minarets Fatimides à la Frontière Nubienne." *Bulletin de l'Institut d'Egypte,* XVII (1934-1935), pp. 141-153.

Kahle, Paul. *Der Leuchtturm von Alexandria.* Stuttgart, 1930.

Karnouk, Gloria. "Form and ornament of the Cairene Bahri Minbar." *Annales Islamologiques* XVII (1981), pp. 15-140.

Kessler, Christel. "Funerary Architecture within the City." *Colloque international sur l'Histoire du Caire.* Cairo, 1969, pp. 257-268.

Kriss, Rudolf. *Volksglaube im Bereich des Islam.* Wiesbaden, 1960.

Lane, E.W. *An Account of the Manners and Customs of Modern Egyptians.* London, 1878.

Makar, Farida. *Al-Sultaniyya.* M.A. Thesis, American University in Cairo, 1972.

Mahmud, .Ahmad. *The Mosque of 'Amr Ibn al-'As.* Cairo, 1917.

Meinecke, Michael. "Die Mamlukischen Faience Mosaikdekorationen: Eine Werkstätte aus Täbriz in Kairo (1330-1355)." *Kunst des Orients,* XI (1976-1977), pp. 85-143.

Pauty, Edmond. "Le Plan de la Mosquée As Salih Talayi au Caire." *Bulletin de la Société Royale de Geographie d'Egypte.* Septembre, 1931, pp. 277-368.

Rogers, J.M. "Seljuk Influence in the Monuments of Cairo." *Kunst des Orients,* VII (1970-71), pp. 40-68.

al-Sa'id, Labib. *al-Adhan wa'l Mu'adhdhinun.* Cairo, 1970.

Salmon, Georges. *Etude sur la Topographie du Caire - La Kal'at al-Kabsh et la Birkat al-Fil.*
Cairo, 1902.

Schacht, Joseph. "Ein Archaischer Minaret-typ in Agypten und Anatolien." *Ars Islamica.* V (1938), pp. 46-54.

Shafi'i, Farid. "The Mashhad al-Juyushi: Archeological Notes and Studies." *Studies in Islamic Art and Architecture in honor of Professor K.A.C. Creswell.* Cairo, 1965.

al-Shafi'i, Farid. "Ma'dhanat Masjid Ibn Tulun - Ra'yun fi Takwiniha al-Mi'mari." *Majallat*
kulliyat al-Adab, XIV/1, 1952, pp. 167-82.

Thiersch, Hermann. *Pharos, Antike, Islam und Occident; ein Beitrag zur Architeckturgeschichte.* Leipzig, 1909.

Van Berchem, Max. *Materiaux pour un Corpus Inscriptionum Arabicarum.* Cairo, 1894.

Yusuf, Ahmad. *Jami' Ibn Tulun.* Cairo, 1917.

Yusuf, Ahmad. *Jami' Sayyidna 'Amr Ibn al-'As.* Cairo, 1917.

Wiet, Gaston. "Sultan Hasan." *La Revue du Caire.* June 1938, pp. 86-109.

Williams, John Alden. "The Monuments of Ottoman Cairo." *Colloque international sur l'Histoire du Caire.* Cairo, 1969, pp. 453-466.

c) Travellers and Artists

d'Avennes, Prisse. *L'Art Arabe d'après les Monuments du Cairo.* 1877.

Breydenbach, Bernard de. *Les Saintes Péregrinations.* Cairo, 1904.

Ĉelebi, Evliya. *Siyahatnamesi: Misir, Sudan Habes,* (1672-1680) Vol. X. Istanbul, 1938.

Coste, Pascal. *Architecture Arabe des Monuments du Caire.* Paris, 1839.

Fabri, Félix. *Le Voyage en Egypte.* 3 vols. Cairo, 1975.

Frith, Francis. *Egypt, Sinai and Palestine.* London, n.d.

Hay, Robert Esq. *Illustrations of Cairo.* London, 1840.

Miquel, A. "L'Egypte Vue par un Géographe Arabe du IV/Xe Siècle: Al-Muqaddasi." *Annales Islamologiques* XI (1972), pp. 109-139.

Nassiri Khosrau. *Relation du voyage de Nassiri Khosrau,* ed. Charles Shefer. Paris, 1881.

Prangey, Girault de. *Monuments Arabes d'Egypte, de Syrie et d'Asie Mineure.* Paris, 1846.

Roberts, David. *The Holy Land - Egypt and Nubia.* 3 vols. London, 1842-1849.

Alphabetical Listing of Minarets in the Survey

(Numbers in italics refer to Figures; numbers in bold, to Plates.)

Produced by the Printshop of the American University in Cairo Press